D0849520

# BRAG BETTER

# BRAG BETTER

## *Master the Art of Fearless Self-Promotion*

MEREDITH FINEMAN

PORTFOLIO / PENGUIN

PORTFOLIO / PENGUIN
An imprint of Penguin Random House LLC
penguinrandomhouse.com

Most Portfolio books are available at a discount when purchased in quantity for sales promotions or corporate use. Special editions, which include personalized covers, excerpts, and corporate imprints, can be created when purchased in large quantities. For more information, please call (212) 572-2232 or e-mail specialmarkets@penguinrandomhouse.com. Your local bookstore can also assist with discounted bulk purchases using the Penguin Random House corporate Business-to-Business program. For assistance in locating a participating retailer, e-mail B2B@penguinrandomhouse.com.

ISBN 9780593086810 (hardcover)
ISBN 9780593086827 (ebook)

Printed in the United States of America
1 3 5 7 9 10 8 6 4 2

BOOK DESIGN BY TANYA MAIBORODA

*For Patti and Dave Nathan,*
*Mort and Jean Fineman,*
*and Joe Nathan*

# Contents

## Part 3
## Going Pro

Dear Reader,

At this point in my career, I've worked with, trained, and spoken to hundreds, if not thousands, of people, many of them women, who find it difficult to talk about themselves and their accomplishments. Actually, "difficult" is an understatement. Most of them find it downright excruciating—it pains me to say that I've had clients who are unequivocally outstanding in their fields, and yet they can't even muster the courage to say their names out loud.

If you're anything like my clients, you do a lot of hard work that goes unnoticed. You watch as colleagues with louder personalities snag promotions, leadership positions, and exciting projects. A chosen few seem to have the magical ability to speak freely, to be heard and acknowledged, and it bugs you that life isn't closer to a meritocracy.

As much as I'd like to say we can get the loud people to be quiet, I don't think that will happen. As a society, we are mixed up about who deserves attention and praise—we reward loud. But we can get the quiet people to be louder by encouraging them to take healthy pride in their accomplishments and by stating true facts about their work for all to hear. That's what I'll teach you in this book.

If speaking up for yourself and those around you makes you nervous, you are not alone. If it were easy, I wouldn't have the career that I do. I should add that this particular insecurity isn't distributed equitably. Never having had proper role models of healthy pride can (temporarily!) set you back. Your gender, race, sexuality, age, ability, and childhood experiences also affect your relationship with bragging. For some of us, bragging is met with more criticism and scrutiny. The freedom to be heard is intertwined with privilege. Throughout this book, you will find callout boxes, brag breakdowns, and quotes taken from one-on-one interviews that I have conducted. You'll hear from people who experience difficult and complex working and social environments and how they've fought to be heard. As a white, cis, straight woman, I'm well aware of the privilege I have, and I'm committed to paying it forward—and I hope you will be committed to the same goal of elevating everyone around you.

My goal is to help you Brag Better—to find the words to describe your work and then share and leverage your accomplishments, in a meeting or from a stage, so you can propel your career forward. I'm confident not only that your accomplishments are worth talking about, but also that sharing them strategically and thoughtfully will help you get farther in your career and in your life.

My deepest wish for you is that, by the end of this book, you feel proud of yourself and your work, and that you have the skills to brag about your unique qualities and experiences, bridging the gap between you and the spotlight. More than anything, the goal of *Brag Better* is to give you a mindset. I want you to know that your accomplishments are enough. *You* are enough. And no matter where you are in your career, your achievements are worth sharing. So, let's start talking about them.

Yours in bragging,
Meredith Fineman

## Part 1

# THE BASICS OF BRAGGING BETTER

**In Part 1, we'll learn how to lay the foundation for Bragging Better. You'll learn why bragging is so difficult and why you shouldn't beat yourself up if you don't know how to do it yet (feeling guilt about being unable to share your accomplishments is a total waste of time). With the three-part formula I'm about to share, you'll have a place to start and plenty of examples to help you see what's possible. By the end of this section, you'll have a new perception and understanding of what it means to Brag Better.**

# 1

# The "B" Word

A few years ago, a thoughtful, personable, and talented client came to me wanting to determine why she felt consistently underestimated. Let's call her Nina.

Nina was tired of feeling invisible in rooms and being passed over for opportunities she felt that she deserved. She did deserve them—it was dead obvious. Like the majority of my clients, she was a member of The Qualified Quiet: a group of highly competent individuals who are underestimated because they lack a strategy for self-promotion, thinking their work will speak for itself. Well, it does not.

Nina was a star. She knew the material backward and forward, in this case politics—she reported on specific demographics and representation. Nina knew her stuff. She had worked harder than most to get a semipopular newsletter off the ground. She clocked sixteen to eighteen hours per day but wasn't taking any of this time to step back and talk about her work, either online or offline. She was stuck in the weeds—and it's easy to get there—analyzing dozens of political races and putting together briefs and research.

Like most of The Qualified Quiet, she was working too hard on the product and not enough on the presentation. When Nina promoted her work, she didn't highlight her credentials and accomplishments, nor did she showcase her witty sense of humor, which made her more engaging than most of the other dry pundits out there. Nina made the mistake of focusing only on the "work" she produced, not realizing her assets included her personality. She also had a star quality about her, one that is difficult to describe but you know when you see it.

At the time that Nina came to me, she was struggling to get on TV. She had done some past appearances, but she wanted to be a more familiar face, someone who viewers cared about. For Nina, TV made sense as a next step to sharing her knowledge—not only to grow her newsletter, but also to cement her status as a political authority. And the idea of shaking up the boring panels we're used to seeing on TV was appealing, too. I knew Nina was capable of it. I don't often say that, because TV is the hardest form of media to secure and on which to perform well.

Nina and I had to tell her story and show the world just how exceptional she was in order to elevate her work. Our time together focused on maintaining her already outstanding newsletter and also creating a focused and thorough personal website. We updated all of Nina's bios to assure that they were consistent and strong. We got her new headshots. We also worked on boosting her confidence about herself and identifying any limiting beliefs that held her back from sharing freely about her accomplishments. Nina wanted to be a star, so she had to think and act like one.

As we did this tactical work, I started to badger TV producers about using Nina as an expert. It's notoriously hard to break into TV, as television appearances are fickle (easily canceled, moved, or "bumped"). Most people aren't going to be good on television, and a booker who secures the talent rarely takes a chance on an unknown.

However, I *had* to get Nina into the rotation. I sent Nina on trips to New York and told bookers we would "be in the area" and available for television. (I mean, *technically* we would be, because I had her travel there, a tactic I still use with a big cheese I want to meet. It only takes a flight or a train to be "in the area.") I know producers are more likely to book someone who is local. So, I made her local. We started getting traction, but it was slow going. Nina smiled her way through junior appearances, including one panel with five people in the audience.

One of the reasons why it was easy to promote Nina was that she had unambiguous goals. She knew her audience, her desired medium, and her message. She knew exactly where she wanted to be. She wanted to be a television commentator, and she knew specifically which shows she wanted to book and that her audience was interested in politics.

A few months later, Nina got her shot.

I will never forget the day that Nina did her first appearance on the show we had been gunning for. As a cord-cutter millennial without live TV, I had to figure out where to watch her appearance. I turned off the sports channel blaring in the roof lounge of my apartment building to the chagrin of the dudes watching it and told them it was time to watch a woman do her thing.

Nina really did her thing. I wasn't surprised, but it went beyond my expectations.

Nina began the segment as a one of several standard commentators. When the host introduced her and asked her a question, she was ready. I watched her rattle off facts and pertinent information at lightning speed. She was armed with her key talking points, but she also took advantage of the short time that was allotted to her by immediately displaying just how deep her knowledge of politics went. The host was taken aback, in a good way, and began to engage with her exclusively for the rest of the segment. The host then began to *ask her* for advice and thoughts. It was by far the best television appearance I had booked to date. It was a magical moment.

Nina told me later that the producers in the control room, the ones behind the cameras calling out the shots and angles, came out to speak to her after the segment—which does not happen, ever. She was that good. These people see commentators every day, and yet they cared enough to stand up and tell her what a good job she had done.

It was a lightning moment for someone who had done the work and was ready to brag about it. Ever since that appearance, Nina hasn't stopped doing the show. She's on that same show at least once a week, as well as many others, and she has grown to be a formidable television presence. She is now so comfortable on TV—cracking jokes, calling out injustice—that she even has entire segments dedicated to her and her ideas.

There are likely many Ninas among you. Even if you don't want to be on TV, even if you never want to stand on stage, you still want to rise in your respective field. You still want to be recognized for your work and respected for your well-thought-out opinions. No matter your goal, *Brag*

*Better* will give you the tools to brag through whichever medium you choose. You already have what it takes to begin, and I will take you to the next level and beyond.

## Redefining Bragging

"Brag" is a dirty word. I'm here to change that. I use it intentionally. I want to get your attention, then show you how to do it.

You are amazing, and I want everyone to know it. I got so tired of hearing people say that talking about themselves "feels bad" or that they are scared people will think "I'm full of myself." I set out to change these sentiments through a decade of coaching, training, speaking, advising, and helping people Brag Better and get what they wanted out of their careers.

When people think of bragging, they often go straight to the idea of throwing themselves a parade. That's one way of bragging. By all means, throw yourself a parade, but that's not what I mean when I say we all need to Brag Better. Bragging Better requires cultivating pride in your work and then taking small actions that help you share it with those around you. To MakeLoveNotPorn founder, international rabble-rouser, and speaker Cindy Gallop, bragging is about "giving yourself credit" and "getting the megaphone out." Gallop believes that hyping your own work is "doing yourself justice" and is necessary to survive.

Being unafraid to speak articulately about yourself, your life, and your accomplishments not only makes you feel great, but also leaves a positive and lasting impact on your listener. I didn't write *Brag Better* with the sole intention of encouraging you. Yes, that's one of my goals, but I want you to feel so good about bragging that you feel free to shout your greatness from the rooftops—and then help your colleagues and friends Brag Better, too.

Bragging Better has nothing to do with pretending—to yourself or to others—that you're more qualified or confident than you are. Knowing how to brag well is different from faking it till you make it, which we all do when it's necessary. And I'm not here to teach you how to insert self-promotion into a conversation at inappropriate times. You won't be learning any tacky gimmicks.

You will, however, find a quiet confidence in your opinions, abilities, and background, and then turn up the volume to share your attributes with your boss, clients, book club, community, neighborhood, and the world. I will help you list your accomplishments and braggable qualities. You will learn how to present the facts of your accomplishments and your highlightable skills in ways that will be best received. I'll share a simple formula for creating an effective brag, and you'll learn the easy actions that you can take to prepare yourself for successful bragging. You'll also learn some next-level tactics.

It's an exciting time to figure out what you stand for and to share it with confidence and conviction.

## The Qualified Quiet

This book is for The Qualified Quiet: those who struggle with or need help finding, feeling, acknowledging, translating, and expressing their amazing abilities, qualities, and accomplishments. In other words, it's for the 99.99999 percent of us who feel uncomfortable talking about ourselves. To some degree, we are all part of The Qualified Quiet. It has nothing to do with introversion or extroversion, but with your reticence to talk about aspects of your life in order to get what you want.

If you have done the work, but you don't know how to talk about and tout it—you're part of The Qualified Quiet. The Qualified Quiet occupy the opposite end of the spectrum from those who brag loudly without focus or adherence to truth. They have experience, but they don't know how to talk about it. They want more than they are currently getting, but they're afraid to say so.

How will you know if you've "done the work"? Even if you're having difficulty identifying it, I promise you have already done a lot of work. (By the way, "loud" people without the hard work background never question whether they have done the work.) That doesn't mean there aren't common benchmarks you can use to determine "work," just so you get an idea:

- You have something to say about your work and your area of expertise.
- You've spent years studying and working within your area of expertise.
- You feel like you know much more than others who are getting more recognition.
- You are in a leadership position of any kind within your team or your company.
- You have an advanced degree in your field (or even a different field).
- You've spoken on a panel regarding your expertise.
- You're a resource for reporters on your subject area.

Many forget they have actually achieved many of these goals, often because it's easy to overlook our own accomplishments.

Bragging Better is an ongoing practice, like any other skill. You have to practice being proud of what you've done and sharing it with others.

And if you don't take the time to brag, it can hurt your career. I've seen clients, friends, and acquaintances miss out on big projects because they didn't throw their hats in the ring. I've watched up-and-coming figures pass up career-altering speaking opportunities because they were too nervous to take them on. And I've seen powerhouses miss out on TV opportunities because they didn't feel qualified or didn't feel comfortable in front of the camera. It makes me mad—at the person making the choice, but also at the system that makes it easier to duck out than to stand up (and that only makes me want to work harder to change that system).

Oftentimes, these successful individuals spend their time and focus perfecting the brand of their organization and, ironically, have not invested in their personal brand and communications strategy. This happens often with communications people, which might sound counterintuitive. You can hawk your own clients until you're blue in the face, but doing the same for yourself feels scary and foreign.

Being a member of The Qualified Quiet is a *good* thing. It's not a weakness; it's a strength. We need you. You are essentially the backbone of our society and workforce. We just need to hear from you. You are the majority, not the minority. You are *so* not alone in feeling bad when you talk about yourself. After all, helping people brag about their work is what I do for a living. If we were all good at it, I'd be out of a job.

## Who Are The Qualified Quiet?

### You Might Be a Member of The Qualified Quiet If You . . .

***Have trouble talking about your accomplishments to others.***

You are never, ever alone in any of these feelings. I coach people over this hump every single day. We all have trouble to some degree—nobody is ever a perfect Brag Better case. We can always improve.

***Feel icky when you see someone else self-promote.***

Does someone talking confidently make your skin crawl? Sometimes this can be because you're not used to seeing it. Or because it makes you wonder about how you would go about doing that for yourself.

***Work in an arena of numbers, data, technology, or science, where any work not tied to firm correct answers doesn't exist.***

I see this regularly in fields like research, science, and technology—more specifically, mathematics, chemistry, healthcare development, medicine, engineering, biology, and data science. These are industries where not giving numbers and firm results is unthinkable.

***Want to barf at the thought of giving a speech.***

During every speech I give (and I give them multiple times a month), I am positive I am going to pass out for the first thirty seconds. Of course, I never do. A fear of speaking in public is incredibly common. Just don't let it hold you back from getting what you want.

***Can chat all day about how great your friends are, but when it comes to yourself, you're silent.***

This is true for so many of us. It's so easy to talk about our friends and clients, about how much we love them and what they do for our lives. This makes it even more confusing. You know *how* to hype—you do it all the time—but when it's time to tout yourself, it doesn't compute.

***Have trouble raising your hand in class, even when you know the correct answer.***
Having the quiet confidence to raise your hand and give an answer, whether you're in a classroom or a big meeting, is terrifying. But I want to help you do it anyway.

***Expect your work to speak for itself.***
This is a big one, and one that affects all of us. Your work doesn't speak for itself. Nobody else knows better what you've done or the hours that you've clocked. If you do not share your work with other individuals or audiences, no one else will. If your work is highly technical or hard to explain, you must learn to clearly describe it to others so that your accomplishments can be recognized.

***Won't seek well-deserved credit.***
This happens often if you work in groups or are in a junior or midlevel position and your name is not at the forefront of a project. Receiving credit is a delicate balance between making your team and your boss look good, while also ensuring that your contribution is noted.

Speaking up, and particularly speaking in public, is a very common fear. That fear has affected me and nearly everyone I know. According to a 2012 study, people fear public speaking more commonly than they fear *death*. As I said, in the first thirty seconds of speaking onstage, I panic; I feel convinced I am going to drop dead. And yet here I am, and I'm still alive.

You can get past this fear, even if you feel like you want to run and hide, barf, or disappear (I've heard it all, baby). I've built a business over the last decade helping otherwise smart people figure out who they are and who they want to be to the public. They started out not knowing the answers to those questions, but once they got clear, they've gone on to win corporate board seats, present TED Talks, and reach exciting goals that they've set for themselves. I'm going to share proven plans for effectively hyping your accomplishments and reaching your own goals.

## You Have to Champion You

Fern Mallis—"Godmother of Fashion," founder of New York Fashion Week, industry consultant, host, and author of *Fashion Lives*—says it perfectly, "Toot your own horn, because there aren't always people who toot it for you." Your work won't be recognized unless you champion it. If you can't champion your own work, neither can anyone else.

*Brag Better* will take you through your own journey to find and elevate your voice. It will illuminate the current environment that does not prime us to champion ourselves, and it will give you a road map to do so using tactics and exercises that I have refined over the past decade. All the tactics in this book have been rigorously tested, both on myself and those I work with. Keep in mind:

- You are far more ready than you think.
- Getting your name into conversations to propel yourself forward is crucial.
- You are there because you deserve to be.
- Your achievements are worth talking about.
- You can land that job, you can secure that promotion, you can get more money, you can feel better about your job, and you can feel seen.

*Brag Better* will do that for you.

I want you to be loud and proud about what you've accomplished, but I also want you to be strategic. You need to have a plan for promoting yourself, and you need to understand what it means to Brag Better.

## The Three Pillars

The three pillars of Bragging Better are to be proud, loud, and strategic. These ingredients get you where you want to go in your career. While that next career step means something different for each person—a new job title or fund-raising for a startup—it will help propel you to the next phase of kicking butt. And don't worry about timing. It's simultaneously never too early and never too late to Brag Better. Start where you are and iterate from there. We are all works in progress, so lacing up and starting now is a great place to begin.

### BE PROUD

This is the essential first pillar of Bragging Better. You need your enthusiasm and your pride. This goes beyond stating your achievements or promoting yourself within a work environment—you need to treat your accomplishments as the facts that they are. If you're not enthusiastic about your achievements, nobody else can be. If you're not there yet, you'll get there. But for now, stand strong in your convictions and your work, and you will eventually convince others, too.

Repeat to yourself over and over again that *bragging is simply stating facts*. You published an article in a big publication: fact. You contributed significantly on a panel: fact. You landed a big-name client: fact. You clearly stated your message in an important meeting: fact. It's easy to believe we haven't done anything of significance, but we're focusing on the facts of your work, your accomplishments, and your life. This is all rooted in firm reality. Your brags will be based on real events, which makes them far easier to share. You'll be reframing your fear and building a list of facts and accomplishments, which can make bragging a lot easier.

Plus, you've gotta do this for our society and world. Please. We have gotten so far away from facts that rooting yourself in the real, tangible, and evidence-based world is helpful not only for bragging but for our conservation of truth.

## BE LOUD

When I say "loud," I'm not referring to the actual volume of your voice. "Loud" means consistently sharing and advocating for yourself and your work. It also means using your voice to help other people—not just yourself. People won't know who you are, what you're about, what you want, and what you need unless you tell them. You have to lay it out. Purposeful volume will get you farther than you ever imagined.

Your employer, your clients, your friends, your colleagues, and your boss all need to hear from you. You're shooting yourself in the foot by not speaking up. You're also doing a disservice to the people you work with, your company's product, or your message when you stay quiet. You are valued because of your point of view, so you need to share it. And frankly, that's part of your job and the reason you were hired.

## BE STRATEGIC

If visibility doesn't align with your bigger life goals, there's no point in going after it—it's just more noise. You have to channel your brags in a way that strategically reinforces your goals.

Your keen sense of your goals is what keeps you focused for success. According to tech revolutionary Steve Jobs:

> People think focus means saying yes to the thing you've got to focus on. . . . It means saying no to the hundred other good ideas that there are. You have to pick carefully. I'm actually as proud of the things we haven't done as the things I have done. Innovation is saying "no" to 1,000 things.

Knowing what you want to get out of your brags is essential. What do you want? What are you gunning for? Don't worry—we will break down those big, life-altering questions. Maybe you are working toward a speaking gig or that big promotion, or maybe you're simply hoping to talk to your boss about the hard work you've done. Maybe you just want to be able to introduce yourself or raise your hand in a meeting without sweating through your shirt. Having a strategy will also help you identify your audience and meet them where they are, so they can better absorb your message. Your strategy drives your brags and helps you get what you want.

## What Does It Mean to Brag Better?

### Bragging Better Is . . .

***Using facts to shine and tell the truth about the work you've done.***

I tell anyone who will listen: If you've done the work, you're only sharing the facts. And it's crucial that we stay committed to truth. We live in a time where what's real and what's "fake news" is muddled. You are here to set the record straight and to show others that the truth matters. I want you to radiate with pride. No matter the accomplishment, there's a better brag for it.

***Having confidence in yourself and your voice: not letting anxiety or self-consciousness get in the way.***

Bragging Better builds your confidence in what you bring to the table and in sharing your value. Your voice is valuable—epically so—to you, your employer, your friends, and your future. Through this process, that self-consciousness will give way to a stronger you.

***Speaking up: not only when it matters, but also when it benefits those around you and helps raise all voices.***

Bragging Better is not just for your benefit. Your ability to confidently share your work will inspire those who are afraid to raise their voices, too. It's also part of your responsibility to think about how you can showcase the voices of the people who have also done the work and deserve recognition. We cannot do it all ourselves, and paying it forward is gratifying and does a true service to others, whether we know it or not.

***Having a practiced delivery, whether online or offline: knowing what you're going to say, how you're going to say it, and what you're going to do with it.***

You are here to brag, and that takes a lot of practice. Everything and anything worth having takes time, effort, and training. It's a muscle you will learn to flex, but you have to hit the gym and do some reps. Whether you're in front of the mirror, a friend, or a work bestie, understanding not only what you're going to say but how to say it is the key.

***Being concise and clear with your brags: coming up with specific, catchy vocabulary to describe yourself and your accomplishments.***

Specificity is the key to helping someone latch on to your message and understand you. Being creative and having fun with it will make you memorable. Not only will you be confident, but you will no longer feel like a stiff, overly rehearsed robot. What fun is that? You can have fun being you.

***Knowing who you are and how you want to be perceived.***

Most people don't consciously choose how they want to be perceived. Part of my job is to nudge people to make big-picture choices. It requires that we step back and think about who we want to be at work. It isn't easy; in fact, it can be terrifying. But sitting with those thoughts around what you really want to be known for and what you want to inspire when you walk into a room sets you above the rest. The majority of people don't and won't take the time to think through these concepts.

***Having clear goals for bragging: knowing where you want your brags to land and having a firm grasp of what achieving these goals will mean for you and your career.***

Goals make you work harder, more thoughtfully, and with clarity—whether you want to talk about a project, land a speaking gig, or share online. No matter how small that goal is (raising a hand in a meeting or sharing something you wrote with a friend), it's a win. It should be clocked and celebrated. Part of Bragging Better is also celebrating yourself and seeing how far you've come.

***Making clear requests for others to promote you with intent and gratitude: being kind in your requests to help others help you, as well as guiding them through it.***

Fundamentally, people want to help you succeed. But you have to tell them how, where, and when to help you. Otherwise, they are unsure of what to do and only have their own ideas of what help means. Define help for yourself and ask that of others. It's a vulnerable act to ask for help, but it will show others that asking for help is not only important but admirable and doable.

## Bragging Better Is NOT . . .

***Fabrication or exaggeration: share about what you've done, and never lie about it.***

Lying is not productive, nor is it necessary. It undermines your integrity and the integrity of those associated with you. Check yourself if you're feeling inclined to lie. Your accomplishments, as they are right now, are enough. They don't need to be exaggerated to land well and Brag Better. It's the *how* of the brag, not the *what*.

***Volume without focus: being loud without strategy is useless, will only damage you, and cannot further your goals.***

You can always get attention by being the loudest in the room, literally or metaphorically, but volume is useless if you're in the wrong room. In other words, being loud but lacking strategy will do more harm than good. When you learn how to Brag Better, you will know how to strategize and strike when the opportunity arises. By channeling your message, you are aligning your past accomplishments, expertise, and hard-won victories with what you want to achieve, learn, and gain in the future.

***Always asking others to promote you without returning the favor: bragging is a two-way street, and the best part comes from your understanding how important it is to let others brag, too.***

Asking people to brag for and about you is an important skill to cultivate. Understanding how and when to ask and when to offer to brag on behalf of someone else is just as powerful. Sometimes choosing not to brag about yourself is the right move. By promoting someone else and letting them shine, you reinforce the idea that everyone can win.

***Preventing others from shining along with you: there is plenty of space for everyone's unique accomplishments, and jealousy will only hold you back.***

It's easy to be jealous. Our modern world feels designed to make you feel inadequate, with a constant feed of beautiful, happy images of seemingly perfect lives, curated to a T. It can feel awful, but it's also not real. Coming to that conclusion takes a lot of time and self-control. Jealousy holds you back more than anything else. It causes you to miss the beauty in your own life.

***Using harmful language: punching down or insulting others to get your brags across defeats its entire purpose.***
As you rise, your friends rise will rise, too. Insulting the work of others or putting someone down to get where you want to be might feel good in the moment, but in the long term, it's bad practice and bad energy. It's not what you want to put out into the world; do unto others as you would have them do unto you. Be a good example—you never know who is following your lead.

***Negativity about yourself and your work: cutting out qualifiers about yourself and putting yourself down.***
We are often meanest to ourselves. I have said much meaner things to myself than anyone else has ever said to me. We are our own toughest critics, and doing the work to change our self-talk is some of the hardest work we can do. Healthy criticism and a tight, focused lens on your work are important. Being mean to the person who does the work—you—is not.

These are the rules of the road. You can refer to them whenever you need to, throughout this book, in your daily life, or when you're tempted to be mean to yourself or jealous of others. They are a guiding source of what to do and what not to do. Not gospel, but bumpers on the bowling lane of your brags.

## I'll Lead the Way and Show You How

I've made it my mission to change the system that rewards loud and unqualified people. However, I want to make this clear: When we begin Bragging Better, the wage gap won't magically disappear, and the world's most marginalized voices won't suddenly be well-represented. That would be too much pressure on you, dear reader. But by raising your voice and learning to speak for yourself and others, you put pressure on the system in which you play and begin to change it, little by little.

I saw this broken system play out at the junior level with young people, particularly women, who applied to intern for my company, FinePoint. When asked about their experience, these young people gave responses that were uneasy and self-deprecating. I saw it with my friends who were shy about speaking up about their accomplishments. I found myself playing their publicist, but I wanted them to learn how to do it for themselves. When I worked with clients, I saw that even those at the highest levels—CEOs, politicos, tech mavens, and product geniuses—didn't know how to Brag Better. So, I set out to change that. Few have tackled these issues. And that makes the effort hard, but I keep working at it and spreading the message.

Over the past decade, I've trained hundreds of people through FinePoint on their visibility, voice, personal brand, and profile. The vast majority are leaders in startups, brands, or companies that come to my doorstep without a firm idea of who they are and who they want to be online and offline. I have designed and held hundreds of workshops that teach people about their voice and how to use it. I have spoken at hundreds of companies, colleges, and events, reminding audiences that what you have done matters, is worthy of merit, and is really important to share.

By Bragging Better, you will add to a culture of healthy pride. Cultivating the ability to raise your voice and brag for yourself and others is simply training yourself to talk about your achievements, skills, and qualifications—without downplaying them or playing at false modesty. Whether you're just starting out in your career or you're a well-established thought leader quickly rising to the top, *Brag Better* will help you rephrase the conversation around your accomplishments and successfully cut through the noise.

You aren't going to have to dig that deep to find reasons to Brag Better. You will discover that you have dozens of wonderful things to brag about. You, The Qualified Quiet, are ready and able to do this work. Just like many, if not all, of my clients, you have everything going for you, and everything to gain by doing so.

## Ready, Set, Go!

- **What do you feel when you hear the word "brag"? If you still have a negative feeling about the word, remember that you have to be the champion of you. Getting your name into conversations to propel yourself forward is crucial. You are there because you deserve to be. Your achievements are worth talking about. You can land that job, you can secure that promotion, you can get more money, you can feel better about your job, and you can feel seen.**
- **Are you a member of The Qualified Quiet? Know where you are on your Brag Better journey so that you can see your progress along the way.**

# 2

# Why Is Bragging So Hard?

Bragging is hard because *staying quiet is easy*. And who doesn't want things to be easy? Choosing to do the hard work takes a lot of guts, but this is a muscle you need to flex. You might worry that by bragging, you become a target. You're putting the spotlight on yourself and making yourself vulnerable. As humans, we don't want to be vulnerable—it's scary and could lead to pain.

## Bragging Is *Work*

Somewhere along the line, we decided that bragging isn't included in the category called "work." Nine times out of ten a client comes to me saying, "I'd rather just put my head down and do the work than take the time and energy to brag about it." Guess what: *Bragging is part of your work.* A huge part of it, in fact. Doing the actual workload is only a sliver of what it takes to get it seen. Being vulnerable, finding the right words, feeling good about yourself, and projecting confidence—these are all part of your work, and it's necessary to practice doing them well over the span of your career. It's some of the hardest work to do because it feels counterintuitive to what we believe.

"Most women would actually rather minimize their successes than tell people about them," notes Mighty Forces founder and president Amanda Hirsch, citing research she conducted in 2019 with fellow women business owners Jessica Broome and Janet Harris, which examined women's relationship to self-promotion. "At the same time, a majority of women say that they've been inspired by hearing other women talk about their accomplishments. Therein lies the gap: On the one hand, we all say that we benefit from hearing other women speak up, and yet we ourselves don't want to speak up. And not only do we not want to speak up, we would rather seem like less than we are." What she wants to know is, since when did self-deprecation become "good etiquette"? Why do we give away our power in the name of good manners?

Why do you have to go through all this extra muscle-flexing that feels foreign in the first place? Well, I hate to break it to you, but people aren't psychic. They don't automatically know what you do, what you've done, or what you *want* to do until you tell them. There is an old journalism adage that I often use: "You have to tell people what you're going to tell them, you have to tell them, and then you have to tell them what you told them." (Thanks, Dad!) This idea dates back to Aristotle, who wrote about consistency of phrase, but the quote is from an English preacher in 1908, who talked about how he wrote his sermons. The power of repetition matters.

Thanks to ancient Greek philosophers and early 1900s

preachers, we've known for a long time that you've got to state your case—or in our case, *brag*—loudly and proudly if you want people to sit up and take notice. And yet, for so many of us, a very different idea has become just as deeply ingrained: We should be "humble" about our accomplishments. (And when it comes to women, in particular, "humble" means "quiet.") As best-selling author, speaker, and digital strategist Luvvie Ajayi notes, "We think there's nobility in our silence." And she adds that it's time to stop playing humble and start bragging: "I don't think we're noble by being silent. [We need] to make sure that we get the credit we deserve. Being overtly humble means that we're selling ourselves short."

Many of us grow up without the desire to be in the public eye, but if our work makes a difference in the world (and it probably does), it's important to embrace this aspect of your career. "I don't know that I intended to be a public person," says quantitative futurist and best-selling author Amy Webb. But, to her, Bragging Better is a necessary part of the job when you're doing work that matters to people. "If I'm doing a good job leading the Future Today Institute's research, and if the work matters, and it's valuable, then people are going to want me to talk about it. I view the public-facing side of what I do as a part of my job now," Webb said.

If you're trying to land a competitive internship and you don't come up with specific, catchy vocabulary to describe yourself and you don't cut out qualifiers when you mention your accomplishments, that amazing opportunity may not materialize the way you hoped it would. If you're a photographer, your clients might not understand that the hours and hours you spend painstakingly color-grading every photo will make them look more joyful and well-balanced. If you're fund-raising for a startup and don't showcase the promise of what you're building succinctly, smartly, and with poise and directness, you can't plant the seeds you need to get the money. People are busy, and they need to be taught how to appreciate quality and the work that you do behind the scenes. You need to brag about your abilities if you want to get paid and appreciated appropriately.

And it's not just about promotions and leadership positions. Says Mighty Forces founder Amanda Hirsch:

> If more women stepped up and owned their stories—if they declared in a bigger way who they are and what they're up to in the world—it would shift our collective sense of what's possible for women to achieve. If more women leaders, in particular, took the time to share their professional stories, it would create a world where it feels more possible for women to lead in government, in business, in entertainment, in technology, in every area. We could finally get past the default image of a leader as an old, white man.

## We Reward Loud

Our economy and media place disproportionate value on volume. Especially in America, we reward loud. We have a terrible inverse relationship between volume and merit. And guess what—it leads to unfair outcomes. Take a look at any industry, and you'll see someone on the cover of a magazine or giving a conference keynote who isn't necessarily the most qualified candidate but the one who is very good at promoting his or her work and skills. It's rarely the person with the longest résumé or the most degrees spouting their opinions on a highly visible platform, but the person who is unafraid to get out there and say it. Take a look at who we reward with money, power, and the presidency.

## LOUD TRUMPS MERIT

The loud voices who have figured out how to game the system are less incentivized to, you know, be great at what they do. They have figured out that they don't even need to be great, because everyone else is too busy questioning themselves, afraid to speak out.

On top of the pain and shame inflicted on an ignored and undervalued individual, society is facing the broader consequence of living in a non-meritocratic society. We aren't getting all the information we need, whether it's from the world's science, economics, media, or law industries (or any industry, for that matter) because of who is doing all the talking. For too long we have paid attention to the wrong people because of their volume and showmanship.

## THE WORST OF BRAGGING: CRIME

For proof of our obsession with scammer culture, bravado, and those who lie, look no further than the poster child of toxic volume, former Silicon Valley darling Elizabeth Holmes, who was set to be the new icon for women in STEM (Science, Technology, Engineering, and Mathematics) and entrepreneurship. For many women, particularly those in business, Holmes was a beacon of what was to come. She was powerful, unusual (she rode around Silicon Valley on an elliptical bike and didn't eat solid meals), and a self-made billionaire with technology acumen that stacked up to anyone in the old boys' club. Elizabeth Holmes was on every magazine cover, from *Fortune* to the *New York Times*, and was called "The Next Steve Jobs" by *Inc.*

Except Theranos, Holmes's "game-changing" startup, was a scam. It didn't work, and its downfall has been chronicled almost as much as Holmes's rise. She created a deification of herself that lent to nonstop press and money, but without the work behind it to make it truly successful. And she was playing with people's lives. This wasn't just another app; she was creating healthcare technology that was supposed to be a better alternative to current blood-testing methods. That's terrifying.

Theranos isn't the only example of loud, fraudulent enterprises. Enron's CEO also graced magazine covers. Both of these companies were leaders in their field with loud figureheads, but they lacked the foundation to back their perceived success. Even more extreme was their illegal behavior to get ahead. These are two highly unusual examples, but they show that we are willing to believe the person talking the loudest. We are conditioned to believe people.

So, what do we do instead? How do we get the loud people to be quiet? Well, we don't. We need The Qualified Quiet to be louder, and we need to persuade the loud ones among us to share the microphone. For too long we have had "experts" without the experience, and visible commentators, speakers, or leaders who haven't put in the work. The Qualified Quiet have put in the work and now need to brag about it—that is, they have to raise their voices and share their accomplishments. You, as a member of The Qualified Quiet, have a lot to brag about. So why is it such a struggle?

## I've Heard It All

Here is just a teeny-tiny snippet of what my clients and audiences have told me over the past decade:

- "I'm afraid/scared/ashamed/nervous/anxious."
- "What if I seem like a jerk?"
- "I met someone once who bragged a lot and I hated them, so I don't want to be anything like them."
- "I don't know enough."
- "What if everyone hates me?"
- "There is someone who knows more than I do."
- "What if nobody cares?"

As founder of BRAVA Investments and author of *Leapfrog* Nathalie Molina Niño points out, others are resistant to bragging for a much more deeply felt reason: They see bragging as a shortcut. She tells me:

> Women, especially women of color, had a really negative response to the word "shortcut" [for use in my book, *Leapfrog*]. The word that they most associated [with it] was "cheating." That's what I think of when I think of how we Brag Better: acknowledging the internalized trauma that a lot of us feel when we are used to people making us feel like we only got that job because we were the affirmative action candidate. Or there was a quota. Or you're the token woman in the room and, therefore, you got this position more easily than other people. We are so used to hearing and feeling [this diminishment] that we won't take the efficient shortcut."

And in many ways, isn't that what Bragging Better is? An effective and efficient way to call attention to our work, our accomplishments, our genius, and our *impact*? It's certainly quicker than waiting for someone else to take notice—which is what I'm doing if I decide to "let my work speak for itself."

Molina Niño encourages us to do the opposite. "We need to unapologetically embrace that idea of the leapfrog. Of the shortcuts," she says. "Anybody with power, influence, and, let's be honest, capital got there because they took some fricking shortcut. Even if it was an unconscious one—like they just happened to have been born in Beverly Hills and not the South Side of Chicago. That's a shortcut. We have ground to make up. And so, in making up that ground, we better take the shortcut." We had better brag.

## "I FEEL LIKE A FRAUD"

Imposter syndrome—the feeling that you're a fraud and that everyone will find out that you're not who you say you are—is deeply tied to the fear of bragging. It's a cousin. They're both about shaky self-worth, aversion to vulnerability, and a lack of confidence. They're also both just feelings—real, but not true. Impostor syndrome and a fear of bragging convince us that we are unworthy of our jobs, unworthy of recognition, or unworthy of praise. To go even deeper, these feelings highlight the great universal fear that our lives or work don't have meaning.

Though we talk about imposter syndrome a lot now, the term was first coined back in 1978 in an article called "The Impostor Phenomenon in High Achieving Women: Dynamics and Therapeutic Intervention" in the journal *Psychotherapy: Theory, Research, and Practice*. One of the study's authors,

Dr. Pauline Clance, regrets framing it as a psychological problem and not a human experience. "If I could do it all over again," Clance told *Slate*, "I would call it the impostor experience, because it's not a syndrome or a complex or a mental illness, it's something almost everyone experiences."

Don't be fooled: Nearly everyone struggles with low self-esteem (well, everyone who is introspective, self-critical, and holds herself to a high standard—a.k.a. most women, and probably you, reader). Every so often (okay, very, very often) I wonder if today will be the day that the jig is up, that people will realize I have no idea what I'm doing. I think about this all the time, as do many of us. While it's always good to keep yourself in check, it's time to leave your imposter syndrome behind. Bragging can help you do it.

When you stay rooted in your experiences, your know-how, and your expertise, you come to realize that those fraudulent feelings are simply ghosts of anxiety. If you stay in the facts and own your expertise, a lot of these feelings of doubt disappear.

## "WHAT IF I SOUND AGGRESSIVE OR OBNOXIOUS?"

There are good reasons to be concerned with how you sound. These concerns are not unfounded—especially if you're a woman. I'm sure each of us has a story or outside comment from our past that reminds us to pay attention to how we sound. Mine came in the form of criticism that I used "like" too much in a TV interview. And being told that I was "so obnoxious" (you didn't whisper this quietly enough!) after introducing myself during an entrepreneurs' dinner. How about that time in high school, when the yearbook editor changed my yearbook submission to tease me for raising my hand frequently in class? I know what this looks like. And it sucks, it *hurts*, and I still remember it, so many years later.

The fear of being called obnoxious haunts both genders, but it's worse for women. Women have long been called "too much." I'm called "too much" or "a lot" all the time. For centuries, women were supposed to look pretty and shut up. Among the maxims listed in "The Good Wife's Guide" in the May 1955 issue of *Housekeeping Monthly*: "You may have a dozen important things to tell him, but the moment of his arrival is not the time. Let him talk first—remember, his topics of conversation are more important than yours."

This notion that women should be quiet is ancient. Cambridge University historian and classicist Mary Beard says that Homer's *Odyssey*, composed around 800 BCE, may be Western literature's "first recorded example of a man telling a woman to shut up." Odysseus's son Telemachus tells his long-suffering but quite capable mother Penelope to "go back up into your quarters, and take up your own work, the loom and the distaff . . . speech will be the business of men, all men, and of me most of all; for mine is the power in this household." No wonder you feel self-conscious speaking up. The idea that a woman wanted things and could vocalize her wants was taboo, and all these years later we're still fighting this construct.

Even your literal voice, if you're a woman, is deeply policed and doubted, making it hard to want to begin speaking in the first place, especially if your voice is in a higher register. A study in *PLoS ONE* found that "men and women preferred female candidates with masculine voices. Likewise, men preferred men with masculine voices. Women, however, did not discriminate between male voices."

We have been trained to like lower voices—so much so that "findings suggest that men and women with lower-pitched voices may be more successful in obtaining positions of leadership. This might also suggest that because women, on average, have higher-pitched voices than men, voice pitch could be a factor that contributes to fewer women holding leadership roles than men." It's frustrating, but I believe this is changing. The societal acceptance of critiquing a woman's voice and how it sounds affects many friends of mine, from podcast hosts to television anchors. I've been standing right next to friends, who regularly appear on TV, when they are recognized then quickly critiqued on their appearance or their voice. Female podcast hosts often receive nasty emails about vocal fry or upspeak (I have), which is just another example of society's general desire to police women's voices.

And it works. Women remaining quiet is historically normative behavior. We are not used to bragging because it is not "normal." As a society, we tend to reject social behavior that is not "normal" even at the risk of progress. This is all old news to me. We could live and die by this precedent, or we could acknowledge that it affects all of us, say "Gee, that sucks," and then move on. I want you to feel validated in having these feelings. But I also want you to rise above them and brag anyway. Bragging is worth it for women. I know this from experience, and I know it from speaking to and training over a thousand people in the past decade.

## "BUT I'M INTROVERTED"

If you're introverted, you prefer deep one-on-one conversations with a small circle, and people tire you out. You aren't alone. Most of us are a mix of introverted and extroverted, and just because you're Bragging Better doesn't mean you can't lean into your introversion.

For best-selling author, introvert expert, and founder of Quiet Revolution Susan Cain, speaking up and speaking out are particular to each person.

So many public speakers are introverts. "We have a real misconception of what it takes and what kind of person it is who succeeds in amplifying a message in an impactful way," she says. "I meet lots of people [on the speaking circuit], and the interesting thing is that by far the majority of them are introverts."

We need to use strategic volume. "To make a name for myself, I have to be outgoing and loud," Cain continues. "There's a way of doing those things [that] feels congruent with who you are: You can be out there in regular media or social media with the mindset that's purely about sharing ideas or, if you're a comedian, being funny. Whatever your thing is, there's a way to do it where you're primarily motivated just by your art or your prompt or your message, or whatever it happens to be."

## "THAT'S JUST NOT WHO I AM"

We carry our "growing pains" and "old stories" and our childhood dynamics around with us, and they can affect our professional lives and our ability to brag. They also affect our work lives in general. I dig into childhood dynamics with clients all the time, and we realize that a deeply imprinted event in the past, like a presentation in middle school that went awry, can stop you from getting out there today.

When I started on this path, I never realized how much

my work with individual clients would delve into the psyche and what they were taught as children. Whether you had a parent who was erratic and you had to temper your behavior to adjust, or you were admonished for speaking a certain way, you carry that into your work and adulthood every day. It's a hard thing to acknowledge and change, but it is possible. Recognizing those patterns and why you're still participating in them can help remove some bragging barriers.

This extends outside the home, too. I was bullied as a kid, and it sticks with me today. I'm not sure why I never shut up, even while bullied. I didn't, and I am lucky. So much pain is inflicted when we are in our formative years, and I hope that you honor some of that in the search for your Brag Better skills and voice.

Your past does not have to stop you from Bragging Better, taking pride in yourself and your accomplishments, and loving yourself along the way. However, these emotional experiences do affect you, and they do take time to understand and heal. Be gentle with yourself, and when you're reminded of past dynamics in your present reality (for example, with people who remind you of others who hurt you when you were young), pay close attention to what you truly need to communicate. You are an adult, and you can move past these roadblocks.

## "THAT'S NOT HOW I WAS RAISED"

Throughout my career, I have found that the size of one's family says a lot about someone's attitudes toward bragging. There are a few ways this can play out, but family size is one dynamic that can make someone turn inward and quiet instead of firing them up. Many of my clients came from big families where they were forced to deal with that dynamic, and they don't like the idea of having to argue for volume and value.

Many of our old stories, particularly around voice, come from what our parents taught us, or didn't teach us, about speaking up. I feel lucky that I have an incredibly vocal mother, one who was absolutely never afraid to speak up or share her thoughts.

This isn't always the case. For many individuals, having a mother or father who was quiet or shy, or who fulfilled traditional gender roles makes them feel anxious about Bragging Better. This can also be derivative of a more traditional household, one where rules like "women should be seen but not heard" continue on into our current narratives about ourselves.

Many clients that come to me with trouble bragging can point to a religious or military upbringing. I lump these together not because they are similar, but because both are immense infrastructures that suppress individual deviance. The military in particular upholds collectivist values, encouraging individuals to sacrifice themselves for their country. The focus is on the group rather than the individual. Serving is a bold and honorable choice, to be clear, but this type of dynamic would make anyone hesitant to brag.

Ultimately, these distinct upbringings aren't weaknesses, they're strengths. Your unique lens and your experiences shaped you into who you are today. When you are Bragging Better, it's standing in that experience and power, sometimes as deep as your childhood, that allows you to empathize, shine, and move forward. Your past is not to be shoved away. If anything, it should be brought into the open because of how it differentiates you.

## "THEY DON'T SEE US"

But what about external obstacles to raising your voice? To being seen and heard? What do you do when the very mechanisms others use to amplify themselves are inaccessible to you? How can you Brag Better when your authority and lived experience are questioned—or your very *existence* is "invisible"?

"Even in marginalized communities we defer to the preference, not the reality," says Imani Barbarin, writer, communications strategist, and disability advocate known by the handle Crutches and Spice. Barbarin points out that one in five people becomes disabled as they age, and Black people and indigenous people of color are more likely to be affected. And yet, "All of our representation of disabled people are white and, specifically, white men. . . . I've had a disabled deaf Black person say, 'A white person told me that they didn't know that there were deaf Black people.'"

Barbarin points out that such invisibility has been ingrained in our culture for decades: "It's only in the last forty years that we've really seen an integration of disabled people in society, and it's still not 100 percent." And integration does not equate acceptance: "I feel a lot of times, our capacity is questioned. *What are you doing here? What are you doing in the room? Isn't there a special space for people like you?* [The] implication is that we shouldn't be in the room or have a seat at the table. And that happens all the time even in very quiet ways."

Such systemic and culturally ingrained barriers to visibility go hand in hand with systemic and culturally ingrained barriers to accessibility, creating a self-perpetuating cycle. "A lot of people downgrade the activism disabled people do because it's not often in person," Barbarin states, "and the reason why is because nobody gives disabled people the space to speak on their own terms and in their own ways. And we're constantly questioned [about] the effectiveness of our methods, even though we're a quarter of the population and we get things churning all the time." She points out that it's so important to find and give others—especially those she refers to as "the marginalized of the marginalized"—the platform to say "I exist."

So, what can you do if you're struggling against such barriers? Brag anyway. Says Barbarin:

> I think the most empowering thing for me has been realizing there's nothing left for me to lose. I'm already being marginalized within the Black community, the disabled community. People can shout at me that I'm wrong . . . but in reality, there is somebody out there who doesn't have anybody to look up to. And we have dealt with a lack of representation, the lack of our own voices being promoted. If you [can] be the representation you always wanted as a child, that you always knew you needed growing up, [do it]. And don't worry about the detractors or the people that will doubt you because they weren't really for you to begin with.

## Cindy Kent: It's Always a Razor's Edge

*For healthcare executive and speaker Cindy Kent, being a Black woman in a corporate atmosphere feels like an impossible tightrope. Throughout her career, Kent has had to be keenly aware of being "too much" or whatever arbitrary standard the corporate world tossed her way.*

"[First,] they're like, 'You got to tone it down, you're talking to the executive leaders too much during meetings.' Two months later, I got the opposite feedback: 'We don't see you, [and] we need to hear your voice more.' It's always this razor's edge that we skate when you, in my case, are a double minority.

"You're strong, and you're powerful, but people don't accept it, don't expect it, or [don't] see it too often, so it makes it [you] even much more of a unicorn—and that's novel. People are going to poke, people are going to gawk, some people are going to be enamored and enchanted and in awe, but you've got to be prepared and expect all of these different reactions. Some of it [boils down to] survival instinct, of being the only one in the room. [I've] got to play bigger because people are going to discount me otherwise."

Bragging gives you power. You'll be in control of your own story and narrative, before anyone can beat you to it. You and you alone dictate your story. You can't control the audience and critics, or systemic factors. But you can position yourself to feel as powerful as possible. It's much, much easier to create the conversation than it is to change it. You are taking the time to establish your own conversation, around yourself, your work, and your goals. I know because I help people do this every day.

When you're first starting out, you will feel doubt. That's totally normal. What I hope is for you to be able to get comfortable in your own power and feel proud enough of yourself to be able to share what you've done—even when society wants to suppress your voice. Even when you're feeling doubt, cultivating the self-awareness to question that feeling and move forward anyway will eventually lead to strong, measured, and powerful messages. In the next chapter, I'll give you some of the words to do so.

## Ready, Set, Go!

- Do you consider yourself an introvert or an extrovert? How does that description inform the way you feel about bragging?
- With which fears do you identify as described in this chapter?
- Write down two or three "rules" you heard as a child about bragging.

# 3

# Be Proud

I had a client, let's call her Kat, who came to me to help her Brag Better around an award and its acceptance speech. Not only was Kat not proud, loud, or strategic, she didn't even believe that she deserved the award. When she told me she felt that she didn't deserve it, it drove me nuts. As much as it was a bummer to hear that, I was glad she recognized the need to get some help around her award speech, which is why she came to me.

I reminded Kat one by one of the accomplishments that brought her to this award: her decades of service, her organizational growth (measured by employees hired, money made, and visibility) as a result of her hard work, her tremendous leadership, and the glowing reviews from those she had worked with. She didn't trip and fall and get this award randomly. It came from twenty hard years of work and spirit. Sometimes helping clients Brag Better means that I simply reiterate their accomplishments back to them, something you can have people around you do. Most of us just need to hear it from someone else before we can believe it for ourselves.

You didn't accidentally fall into your accomplishments, either. You didn't magically snap your fingers into a promotion or a panel opportunity. If that worked, you'd see a lot more people waving wands. You worked hard to earn those opportunities. You deserve to be there, and you deserve to be heard and seen. "People are not doing you a favor by having you work with them," says Luvvie Ajayi. "You are bringing value to the table. Stand in that and know that. I do think a lot of times, we don't really believe that we're bringing something of value to the table, so then we don't stand our ground." You aren't here by mistake—stop thinking that way. Not only is that line of thinking unproductive, but it just isn't true.

When I worked with Kat, I listed her accomplishments as if they had been achieved by a close friend of hers. That way she could hear them objectively. When Kat heard everything she'd done, she was able to see more clearly that she deserved this award, and she was excited to receive it. Because she gave a killer acceptance speech with a strategy around what she wanted, she was also able to gain new business to boot.

## Why Are You Here?

When I begin my work with clients, the first thing I do is get very clear on what it is they want out of our work together, and what kind of emotional blocks might be in the way of them Bragging Better. As I mentioned, much of my work deals with the psychological and emotional patterns we pick up as children and young adults. Without addressing those stories first, we will likely get nowhere. With that in mind, I want you to ask yourself the following questions. Take your time and write down your answers somewhere you'll be able to refer to them.

- Why are you here?
- Why do you want to Brag Better?
- What do you want to be able to do by the end of this book?
- What does the word "brag" mean to you?
- What thoughts or feelings do you experience when you hear or say the word "brag"?
- If the word "brag" brings up negative feelings, how would you describe them?
- What mental images or memories arise with those feelings?
- For each of those feelings and thoughts, can you describe why you might be feeling them and what life experiences those feelings or memories might be associated with? (For example, you might have a negative experience with your family, in your work, with friends, or with a group.)
- Is there anything else from your past that might also inform your feelings about bragging about yourself?
- If those feelings were resolved, what would you be able to do?
- Are there ways that you can start to talk about your work and the work that you've done that might serve you better?
- How can you ask for help in bragging?
- Who can you ask for help?
- What's one thing you can do this week that will lead you to lean in to your discomfort and accomplish the goals you have for yourself around Bragging Better?

Throughout your Bragging Better journey, I want you to refer back to the answers to these questions whenever you feel doubt. Your goal will remind you why you're doing this in the first place, and any stories from your past will remind you why you feel resistance. My hope is that, when you feel doubt about advocating for yourself, your goals will far outweigh any negative memories from the past.

## What Have You Done?

Next, sit down with a pen and paper and make a list of the facts of what you've accomplished. The cold, hard facts. List everything: the small wins, the big accomplishments, the tiny ones that you are proud of and want to celebrate. The list below is partially inspired by Peggy Klaus, the author of *Brag!*, who as the founder of BRAG! Connections empowers women and girls. It's also inspired by my years of work. But don't limit yourself to what I've shared here—if you have other achievements that make you proud, whether personal or professional, write them down.

- List your accomplishments over the last year—at least one per month.
- List your top accomplishments over the past five years.
- Include accomplishments that are outside of work. Are you a board member for a nonprofit? Did you volunteer for a worthy cause? Include anything you did that feels like an achievement.
- List any accomplishments from your previous employers that make you proud.
- Write about the aspects of your personality that you bring into your work. Are you extroverted? Intuitive?

Funny? How does your personality make you better at what you do?

- List the projects you have worked on in the last year that you are most proud of. What makes you proud of your work? What about those projects did you like, and what skills did these projects allow you to use?
- What are you best at in your current position?
- List five regular tasks that you do in your current work that excite you. Get as specific as possible. They don't have to be big tasks, just something you enjoy (for example, I personally enjoy preparing folders for big meetings because it makes me feel organized and in control).
- List what you have learned about yourself and your work in the last year and in the last five years.
- List any new skills, abilities, certificates, or degrees that you have acquired in the last year or in the last five years.

You will see that you have already done so much more than you realize. Remember, you decide what counts as an accomplishment. It's not for other people to tell you what qualifies.

List the outcomes of your work, too. How have your accomplishments and your hard work affected those around you? None of this happens in a vacuum: Our actions affect the ecosystems of our workplaces, our communities, and even our groups of friends. If you're having trouble seeing the outcomes, ask coworkers and colleagues, friends, and other advocates. Perhaps a suggestion you made in a meeting brought in more money for your company. That's a huge outcome. Maybe your panel appearance inspired one audience member to reach out to you afterward to tell you how his business was positively impacted. Outcomes aren't about creating change for a thousand audience members—it's a good outcome if it's an audience of one, too.

Don't be afraid to ask your coworkers what they think your strongest attributes are at work. Getting others' perspectives helps you see your own value, and it will also highlight things you might not see as accomplishments. We often don't recognize skills that come naturally to us. Plus, it feels nice to have a bunch of colleagues compliment you.

Here's what some of my clients were proud of when they listed their accomplishments:

- Getting rewarded with a big bonus that made them feel valued.
- Bringing in new business, more than ever before.
- Standing up to a bully at work.
- Doubling their book of business.
- Handling senior leadership and junior hires equally well.
- Landing a highly competitive promotion despite personal challenges at home.
- Nailing the investor pitch.

When asked to list tasks that excite them, they said they like to:

- Pitch meetings with potential clients.
- Run a successful panel for a big-name author.
- Counsel junior employees.
- Break down big tasks into small, actionable pieces.
- Pitch their brand to new faces.

They also talked about what they are best at:

- I can talk any client off a ledge when they're about to erupt about something.
- I am the best in my division at reading the room and figuring out the truth about where we are with a project.
- I am great at asking for help when I need it.

When they asked coworkers, collaborators, or colleagues for feedback regarding the outcomes, they heard:

- You are an unbelievable connector and you make people feel comfortable and seen.
- You were able to handle a difficult client with grace and patience, and you saved us from losing the account.
- You light up a room with your poise and humor—even tense situations are better because of your presence.
- Your extra work on that project made the client so happy that they signed a contract for another two years, which led to hundreds of thousands of dollars of revenue.

## What Are Your Self-Stats?

A great way to identify key office brags is to know your "self-stats," the cold, hard numbers that you can easily use to tout your work. Self-stats are quickly measurable ways to mark the value you bring in the most traditional sense.

- Can you put a dollar value on the work you do? (That is, each project completed, each client handled, each sale closed?)

- How much money do you bring into your department? To the entire company?
- How much is your account worth?
- What large pitches did you contribute to and win?
- How many people do you manage? Is this number up from when you started?
- How many projects have you been asked to spearhead in the last year? Since you started in your current position? Since you started at the company?
- How long have you worked at the company?
- How quickly have you been promoted?

For example, you might say:

- I handle a budget of $1.5 million, which has grown by 25 percent year over year since I stepped into managing the department.
- I handle seventy-five client cases per year, a number that has grown every single year since I started.
- I manage a team of five employees, and I train other managers to do the same.

Keep track of your self-stats. Write each one down, no matter how small you think they might be.

Also consider the context of your accomplishments, as they matter sometimes more than the actual job well-done. Did you manage to keep your team together in a time of heavy layoffs? Did you manage to keep your expenditures down when every other department had ballooning expenses? Are you the youngest person to be in a vice president role at your firm? Or conversely, have you put in two more decades than anyone else you know?

This is also a good place to consider the direct outcomes of your work, like "My work at the shelter increased senior dog adoptions by 200 percent in the first year." The numbers are difficult to argue with (and everyone loves dogs).

## Constructing Your Brags

When it comes to framing your achievements as facts, keep your statements simple. Use as few adjectives as possible, and leave comparisons to other people out of your brags:

- I won this award because I landed three new accounts for my division.
- I earned this promotion because I manage six people, all of whom are happy and thriving.
- I am on this panel because I have a regular column about the industry and I have unique opinions and experience.

Brags can be made up of accomplishments in and out of the office. You're a whole person, not just a corporate robot. That means what you bring to your job, your community, your outside interests, your desires to improve the lives of those around you, or whatever else floats your boat. Often, your hobbies are worthy of brags, too, and they can have more impact than just stating a fact or figure. If you organized a group of coworkers to do a white elephant gift exchange, which was fun and silly, that's something you did that makes a difference to office morale. If you start an initiative to get more of your coworkers volunteering at a soup kitchen you give time to, that's true value you're creating and worthy of recognition.

## LANGUAGE IS OUR MOST POWERFUL TOOL

The most powerful tool that we have at our disposal is language. I probably don't have to convince you of that, but it's worth repeating, because we often don't consciously decide how we want to communicate about ourselves. It is how we communicate, signal success and failure, and interact with the world around us. To Brag Better, we need to create our own language to help us hype ourselves. While I cannot give you the words entirely, there are guideposts that will help.

If you use language in a targeted, thoughtful, actionable, and directed way, the opportunities for you and your work are endless. We are all talking, but are you really considering your word choice and how exactly you're describing your work? It's the difference between having people halfheartedly listen to you and getting them to zero in on what you're saying. The more targeted your impact, the better.

Each word you use matters, and the wrong ones can tank your brag or your business prospects (not to mention misspelled words or names—boy, is that a great way to signal that you're not paying attention). The winning formula here is to combine a consistent message with a tone and word choices that are impactful and uniquely you. Figuring out your ideal communication style takes time, but it makes you someone people want to listen to, pay attention to, and reward.

## SUPERPOWER WORDS

Words are a superpower. Your chosen superpower words will inform the way you talk about yourself. They have a few powers: First, they help you feel good and center your brags. Then, they serve as descriptions that will help you create your brags.

I'll use myself as an example. I care that my voice and my brags are funny, thoughtful, and helpful. I want you to find me hilarious, and I want you to feel that I put a lot of time and effort into my work. But I also want to help you achieve your goals. That's why I chose this combination of three "superpower" words for myself—funny, thoughtful, and helpful. You don't have to have three, but it's a good place to begin. Your chosen words create a framework and an attitude around your voice and will be your ideal way of describing yourself when you Brag Better. I chose these words because that's how I'd like others to see me, but they also further my goal of the voice I want to create.

For each post I make, or story I write, I want to fulfill at least one of those adjectives. I don't have to nail all of my adjectives at one time. I might be funny in one post, and then thoughtful and helpful in another post. I want to ensure that my superpower words are conveyed with continuity over time.

What are three "superpower" adjectives you can identify when you step back and think about your voice and what you want to communicate? On the next page, you can circle or note the adjectives that you want to describe your voice. Which of these pumps you up when you read, say, or hear them? This is a very small sample but will help kick-start your thinking, and they can help when you are in a bragging rut. If I'm ever unsure of how to word a brag, or how to practice a particular introduction, I go back to my superpower words and make sure that whatever I'm trying to communicate matches up with my long-term intention. It's a baseline for consistency, which is one of the keys to success.

Check the box next to the adjective that applies to you, or insert some of your own.

- ☐ Edgy
- ☐ Serious
- ☐ Subtle
- ☐ Professional
- ☐ Graceful
- ☐ Zany
- ☐ Adventurous
- ☐ Brilliant
- ☐ Compassionate
- ☐ Daring
- ☐ Determined
- ☐ Esteemed
- ☐ Fearless
- ☐ Flawless
- ☐ Glamorous
- ☐ Imaginative
- ☐ Kind
- ☐ Major
- ☐ Natural
- ☐ Offbeat
- ☐ Passionate
- ☐ Upbeat
- ☐ Warm
- ☐ Polished
- ☐ Popular
- ☐ Powerful
- ☐ Prestigious
- ☐ Proper
- ☐ Qualified
- ☐ Quirky
- ☐ Radiant
- ☐ Remarkable
- ☐ Regal
- ☐ Respectful
- ☐ Responsible
- ☐ Rowdy
- ☐ Sarcastic
- ☐ Sentimental
- ☐ Smooth
- ☐ Sophisticated
- ☐ Striking
- ☐ Supportive
- ☐ Tender
- ☐ Thoughtful
- ☐ Valuable
- ☐ Whimsical
- ☐ Brash
- ☐ Comfortable
- ☐ Excited
- ☐ Friendly
- ☐ Jazzy
- ☐ Carefree
- ☐ Beloved
- ☐ Bubbly
- ☐ Courageous
- ☐ Decisive
- ☐ Dramatic
- ☐ Fabulous
- ☐ Funny
- ☐ Frank
- ☐ Heartfelt
- ☐ Impressive
- ☐ Knowledgeable
- ☐ Brave
- ☐ Nimble
- ☐ Bold
- ☐ Playful
- ☐ Vibrant
- ☐ Witty
- ☐ Demonstrative
- ☐ Authoritative
- ☐ Trustworthy
- ☐ Worldly
- ☐ Offbeat
- ☐ Ambitious
- ☐ Bossy
- ☐ Candid
- ☐ Creative
- ☐ Delightful
- ☐ Elegant
- ☐ Fancy
- ☐ Flamboyant
- ☐ Genuine
- ☐ Honorable
- ☐ Joyful
- ☐ Lively
- ☐ Memorable
- ☐ Noteworthy
- ☐ Original
- ☐ Trustworthy
- ☐ Vivid
- ☐ Zealous

Remember, you're not married to any of this. You can look at your list and decide to evolve over time. I definitely cared more about whimsy than I did about impact, say, ten years ago. The greater point is to consciously choose the intentions and feelings that you want to communicate consistently over time.

I once worked with a client named Sarah who had written an amazing book but was having trouble promoting it. It was difficult for her to talk about herself because she'd spent most of her career behind the scenes and felt like people who chose to be in the public eye were somehow less trustworthy or truthful. She knew how to cut to the center of a complex issue, so she needed to cut to the center of her voice, too. We decided to describe her skills using three killer words: "soulful," "thoughtful," and "genuine." I told her that from then on, her brags and shares had to tie back to those three keywords, whether it was in phrasing, tone, or feeling. Focusing on those three superpower words helped her feel more authentic and comfortable when taking center stage. She didn't have to adopt a fake persona. As a result, she was able to promote her book and get bigger press and speaking opportunities.

## Verbal Undercutting: What Not to Say

Sometimes, knowing how to Brag Better is knowing what *not* to say. The Bragging Better strategy includes ending any habits you might have of verbal undercutting, or self-sabotage in the form of negative sentiments toward yourself. Aside from the fact that it's hard to be around someone who constantly knocks themselves down, it undermines your work.

There is a fine line between self-deprecation and self-loathing. The former says, "I can poke fun at myself and I am self-aware but still serious," and the second promotes negativity, drives people away, and has the opposite effect. That is a line we can walk together, and one that you will always need to be conscious of. We are all guilty of this, but the more aware of it you are, the more you can remove it from your language.

It also requires some trial and error. During speeches, I often make jokes about my habit of wearing jumpsuits and that I'm there to help the audience Brag Better but also "change their oil." That one goes over well. I am making fun of my outfit but also not totally insulting myself. If you get too self-deprecating, you'll see some grimaces. Sometimes my humor is too dark and, well, it freaks people out. It took some calibration, so don't worry if you mess up at first.

Sometimes verbal undercutting isn't overt. It can be more subtle, but just as damaging. I had a client, we will call her Stacy, who consistently used qualifiers when referring to the work she was doing. In true Qualified Quiet fashion, she had already spent two decades killing it in the retail world, and yet she kept saying she was "trying" to disrupt the industry. She had already spent twenty years doing so. It drove me nuts.

Stacy had created a technology and fashion platform that was in its early stages, but she kept acting as if she hadn't done squat. The word "trying" or "attempting," qualifiers that tell the reader you aren't doing the work, need to be avoided. These qualifiers communicated her hesitancy and doubt in herself to potential users, customers, and even investors. It made them doubt her abilities, too. Had I not known about her talents, I would've thought she was significantly more inexperienced than she was, and I'm not sure I would have taken her as seriously as she deserved.

This is just one example of subtle verbal undercutting. You want to use an active voice versus a passive one to show your activity and forward movement. This goes back to one of our core tenants: *Bragging is stating facts.* So, state them loud and with intention. Stacy created and founded a technology company. Fact. She has two decades in the industry and is full of insider knowledge. Fact. Her product objectively differed from anything else out there. Fact. Don't take yourself out of the running before you've even set foot on the track. You're doing yourself a disservice, and the disservice extends to anyone working for or with you.

A more overt way of undercutting yourself verbally is putting yourself down, even as it directly relates to sharing your brags, which is my ultimate pet peeve. Whether it's a phrase like "shameless plug," "humblebrag" (the worst!), or "I hate to brag, but . . . ," you need to cut it out. Please, for me. These undercuts are less overt than saying "I suck!," but they are just as dangerous, almost undercuts in disguise. It can feel like a reflex—we have all been conditioned to say these sorts of things when we are uncomfortable or anxious, or we feel like we aren't allowed to be proud. That's why Bragging Better starts with a feeling—being proud of and grounded in the work you *have actually done.*

A list of phrases you should never use when bragging:

- Self-promotion alert!
- Shameless plug
- I hate to brag, but . . .
- Shameless self-promotion (This is really a killer as it combines two.)

We are so used to undercutting ourselves verbally that we don't even notice when we do it. When I call it out or yell it on the phone to a client (okay, gently, and with intention), they often have no idea what they've said. It takes another person listening, and now you know to check yourself on this, and how to gently guide a friend when they do it, too.

After a recent Brag Better training presentation, I wrapped up my talk and began the question-and-answer portion. The very first question I got was asked by a woman who began with, "I have a really loud voice and can't stop talking." Even after literally listening to a talk on bragging, it was so ingrained in her to insult or undercut herself that she said exactly what I had warned her against.

I pointed it out immediately. I said your voice is yours, and yours alone, and I like how it sounds just fine. I said it back to her as she had said it to me. I suggested that she imagine me as a close friend and asked what she would say to that close friend. She understood the difference and started again with "I love my loud voice and I have a question." She had flipped the script and led with pride, which made her sound strong and resonant. We all insult ourselves or wear our insecurities on our sleeve sometimes. Ask those around you to watch it for you, too—sometimes it's hard to hear your own speech patterns.

Verbal undercutting isn't a matter of calling someone out. It's to understand when and how we do these things that hurt us. Turn it on yourself in the way you would a close friend or someone you love. It's saying, "I'm flagging that phrasing for you. It sounds like you're insulting yourself, and you have nothing to be ashamed of." When I said that to the audience member, I wanted to make her think, make her feel okay, and not add to her pile of shame. We often are used to saying these things, and it doesn't even occur to us that it might be holding us back. Be sure that the person is ready or willing to hear that feedback. If it's not someone who is open to it, the results will likely backfire and that person will become defensive.

Here's what's happening when you verbally undercut yourself. You're saying that you've accomplished something, but you have no idea how to communicate it in a way that feels good to you and feels good to the reader or listener. Thus, you insult or put yourself down before someone else can. Because of the degree of vulnerability associated with bragging, it can feel scary and uncomfortable. But that is a calculated risk. We are so conditioned to do this that we often don't even notice it. Being conscious of this is half the battle.

This type of language is detrimental to your own self-esteem, but just as important it makes your audience disengage. It makes them wonder whether they should stand behind you, because they can sense the anxiety in your voice and delivery. These feelings transfer to the people you need most—your audience. You want your audience to feel good and to feel strong and know that you are worth listening to, so you have to present yourself as such.

Over the decade I've spent helping those in the public eye, I've found that the chances that someone will insult you are very slim. It's normal to fear—look at our continual mudslinging. But it's less probable than you might think. You don't need to preface discussing an accomplishment with an insult. Women are especially prone to undercutting. Why? Because being a woman who is proud and loud is not only undervalued but also tinged with shame. I see many women professionals verbally ruining their argument by being the first to slam it.

Negative qualifiers actually create negative sentiment for your audience. If I see you post something with "humblebrag alert," it's not encouraging me to champion or help you. Instead, I'm not sure what to do with the information you are sharing and will likely not engage with the post at all. That negative sentiment you feel transfers to your reader. You want to tell your reader or onlooker what they're looking at, and how they can support you. If I am feeling like you cannot support your own accomplishment, then I don't want to champion it, either.

Consider the following suggested replacements:

| Instead of This: | Say This: |
|---|---|
| I hate to brag, but . . . | I'd love for you to read this article I wrote. |
| Shameless self-promotion | Please share this post I wrote on my industry. |
| Brag alert | I'd be so grateful if you watched my most recent TV segment. |
| Plugging myself | Check out this video from a panel I was on! I had a blast. |

There is a huge difference between self-deprecation and verbal undercutting. The first is purposely poking fun at yourself, but not doing so with any bad intent. The latter hurts you—putting yourself down without any humor or levity, and the former can endear you. It's a very fine line to walk, but here are some examples of the difference:

| Scenario | Self-Deprecating | Verbal Undercutting |
|---|---|---|
| Pointing out a fault | Even in college I was always the last one to turn in a paper. | You know me, can't ever get anything in on time. |
| A project | I loved this project and am proud of the outcome—despite Sarah out here making us all look bad with her PowerPoint skills. | I'm glad you liked my work on the project—we all know it was really Sarah who did the best job. |
| An introduction | I run a division of a nonprofit that just saw its highest growth in a decade. Modest, but true. | I hate to be so in your face or whatever, but I run a division of a nonprofit that just saw its highest growth in a decade. |

It's important to understand these distinctions. It's the difference between making people feel close to you and in on your jokes (self-deprecating), versus anxious and isolated from you (verbal undercutting). It's a line you will have to walk continually, and you will make mistakes. But it's how you will learn the difference.

## Ready, Set, Go!

- **Create a list of your accomplishments.**
  - Think about five of your regular tasks that excite you. Get as specific as possible—perhaps it's conversing with clients or developing reports.
  - Ask your coworkers what they think your strongest attributes are at work. Think about these attributes as they relate to the above tasks.
  - Write down the work experience, meeting, pitch, or presentation you are most proud of. What makes you proud of it? What made you enjoy it? Why were you uniquely suited to do it?
  - What are you best at in your current position?
- **Compile your self-stats.**
  - How much money do you bring into your department? To the entire company?
  - How much is your account worth?
  - What large pitches did you contribute to and win?
  - How many people do you manage? Is this number up from when you started?
  - How many projects have you been asked to spearhead in the last year? Since you started in your current position? Since you started at the company?
  - How long have you worked at the company?
  - How quickly have you been promoted?
- **Choose three superpower words that excite you. Practice speaking and writing in a way that can be described by these three words.**

- **Monitor your speech for a day. Do you hear yourself using verbal undercutting phrases? If so, practice the following types of phrases:**
    - I'd love for you to read this article I wrote.
    - Please share this post I wrote on my industry.
    - I'd be so grateful if you watched my most recent TV segment.
    - Check out this video from a panel I was on! I had a blast.

# 4

# Be Loud

Lisa was raised in a conservative family and in an equally conservative small town. Her early life was shaped by traditional gender roles at home and in her community, where passivity was considered feminine and becoming. As a result of these scenarios—a family in which she didn't feel comfortable to speak and a town in which she didn't see strong, vocal women—she found it especially hard to speak up with her ideas.

Despite the background she came from, Lisa wanted to play hardball in her professional life. She got into finance, an extreme men's club. Lisa excelled, but she didn't shout with the stockbrokers or party with the bankers. Although she was in a notoriously difficult arena for women, she was really good at her job.

Her lack of comfort being vocal became more of a problem when she wanted a promotion. Lisa knew she was good, but the industry she found herself in and her background made it very, very difficult for her to advocate for herself. So, after a past client of mine told her about my work, she called me and asked for help.

First, Lisa and I talked about the incredible job she had done juxtaposing her background with the career she found herself in. I told her it was no small feat to go from a small town to the big finance stage. And I'm not sure anyone had ever told her that. Sometimes a huge part of Bragging Better is realizing you were afraid and told not to do something, and you did it anyway.

Then we worked on how she would lobby for her promotion. She began by asking a male coworker who exhibited a lot of the vocal traits Lisa lacked to back her up in meetings and by watching how he talked about his work in group settings. After a few tries, Lisa was able to speak up, adding little by little what she knew. I'd have her write down what she wanted to say. Many of my clients, no matter how senior, benefit from this. You'd be shocked at how much it helps to just have it all written down, even if your notes say, "Hi, my name is Meredith." Having notes stops a lot of panic—I have note cards every time I go on stage.

Lisa had begun speaking up in meetings, but she had to fight very vocal men for a promotion. So, I had her do what you'd do for any other kind of pitch: create a deck and presentation for herself, complete with notes and printouts for her superiors. Lisa also had to start walking the walk of the leadership role she wanted. She had to frame her bios with active prose, purposely display projects where she was a strong leader, and simply describe herself as a leader. She had to lay that groundwork verbally, and then start acting like a leader, too.

When the time came to submit herself for the promotion, Lisa was ready. She had her PowerPoint and her proven work track record written out and framed with her as a leader, and she was able to throw her hat in the ring confidently and proudly. She didn't get the promotion, but her boss noticed the change in Lisa. He told her to keep throwing her hat in the ring for the next rounds of leadership roles, which boosted Lisa's confidence and made her feel as if her boss believed in her.

The next pillar of Bragging Better is being loud. Of course, half the argument of this book is that loud people are getting in the way of you being heard and moving forward. But when I say loud, I mean turning up the volume dial and turning up the frequency. If that means contributing once a week to a meeting, great. If it's writing a quarterly newsletter and promoting it on social media, also great. Volume is relative, and the decibels are up to you. We want to focus on cultivating the feeling of pride in our work and then sharing it with a volume that does our work justice. Getting increasingly louder takes time, effort, and a few skills I'll share with you in this chapter.

Best-selling author and introvert expert Susan Cain encourages being loud in a way that feels true to you. "Can you figure out ways of expressing yourself that feel congruent with who you are and that are going to achieve those goals? It might be things like writing a column or something like that where you're able to showcase what your expertise is and share it. The action that you're taking is still aligned with who you are and what your values are," she says.

For Pat Mitchell, cofounder of TEDWomen, former CEO of PBS, former president of CNN Productions, and author of *Becoming a Dangerous Woman: Embracing Risk to Change the World*, hearing our own voice is essential: "Once we hear our voice, [we] know that it sounds qualified. It sounds experienced. It sounds smart. Because women are prepared. Being prepared, doing the homework, and speaking up are essential." In fact, Mitchell was so eager to get women, especially young women, to speak up in the public sphere that she would hold training sessions and even bribe them to do so by saying, "I'll take you for a drink tonight if you ask the first question." And while some of her tactics may have been lighthearted, her intent was deeply serious. "We ask for raises less often," Mitchell notes. "We put ourselves forward for promotion less often. We feel like we have to be overqualified and over-experienced for every position when we know men don't feel the same."

### Ruth Ann Harnisch: Raise Your Voice for Good

*Ruth Ann Harnisch—professional coach, philanthropist, and Harnisch Foundation founder—knows a few things about raising her voice and the voices of others.*

"Why loud? If you *can* be loud, why would you not want to be loud on behalf of those who have no voice? I do not understand why it's okay with some people to ignore the underrepresentation, the systemic unfairness, the human suffering happening all around. If you think it's important, it's important to get loud about it (strategically)."

## The Power of Being Direct

We can't talk about being loud without first talking about our general fear of being direct. And what I mean by "direct" is this: saying exactly what you mean and acting on what you want. I work with clients all the time who have absorbed the idea that if they are direct, they will be considered bitchy, or rude, or "too much."

I grew up with a mother who is very direct. My mom had (and still has) no problem sharing exactly what she thinks and asking for what she wants. I was fortunate to grow up with a female role model who had none of the conditioning that I see in my clients. I'm direct as a result of my upbringing; it's ingrained in me.

The majority of them, however, are not comfortable being direct and have never had a role model who can show them how to ask for what they want. To some degree, most women have been taught that we must ask nicely for things, that we must beat around the bush, that we have to sugarcoat what we want or feel so that it's palatable for someone else. We're taught to be anything but direct.

So much of being able to Brag Better is cultivating the ability to say what you mean and say what you want—without sugarcoating, without tempering it to avoid someone else's discomfort. Ripping the Band-Aid off, so to speak, is far more effective than dancing around what you really want to say.

For example, I have an incredible friend who started and runs a technology company that employs 150 people. She was on a huge list of the best up-and-coming tech firms, and her work is no joke. She wrote a post to share the accolade, and it started with "I hate self-promotion." I pinged her immediately and we worked on a new post together, one that began with her saying how grateful she was to be recognized. She deeply deserved this accolade, and she deserved to feel good about it, too. This only goes to show how deeply we struggle with being visible, being seen, and voicing our accomplishments. You'll recognize this particular phrase as a form of verbal undercutting. Removing these phrases from your speech is the first step in speaking directly.

Even though I grew up with a very direct mother, I still had to work on my own "stuff" around bragging and speaking up. I've spent ten years working on how to advocate for myself and my work, and for the work of others. I've had to learn how to have better conversations, how to stop avoiding conflict, and how to express clearly what I want and what I've achieved. Before I took this on, I had the habit of dancing around what I wanted to say, and when I didn't succeed, I would get angry with myself over it. I can tell you this for sure: being direct is so much simpler and efficient than doing the avoidance dance.

Let's take a moment to talk about what I mean (and don't mean) when I say "be direct." Too often, people hear the word "direct" and think of the words "blunt" or "confrontational." That's not what I mean here, although I'm not excluding those two approaches from your arsenal of advocating for yourself. Being direct means going from point A to point B without stopping or taking any detours. In other words, you don't need to tell a story, you don't need to justify yourself, you don't need to manage the other person's feelings, you don't need to wait for the perfect time, you don't need to "be nice." You just need to share what you want them to know, clearly and succinctly.

I don't say this lightly—there are massive differences in how women and men share their accomplishments in the workplace. And differences in outcomes, too. One research study showed that men rated themselves 15 points higher on a 0 to 100 self-assessment scale than their female counterparts did when asked to make the same self-assessment. Those who self-promoted were more likely to be hired and at a higher pay.

In another study, researchers analyzed over six million research papers in peer-reviewed medical and scientific journals to study "gender differences in the self-presentation of scientific research." The goal was to assess if papers whose first and last authors were women presented their own findings in less positive terms than the papers whose first and last authors were men—as identified with the use of words like "novel," "unique," and "unprecedented." It's probably no surprise that papers by mostly female researchers were on average 12 percent less likely to use "positive framing" of their findings, meaning they used language that cast their studies in a highly significant light. What's more, papers that use such framing were cited by other scientists about 9 percent more often than were the papers with less positive language. "Since citations are a key determinant in hiring and promotion decisions, gender differences in language use may have tangible career implications," said lead study author Marc Lerchenmueller of the University of Mannheim in Germany. "Women's work may receive less attention and recognition as a result of them using more timid language." In the field of academic medicine, where women already receive fewer promotions, earn lower salaries, and receive fewer research grants than their male colleagues, being shy about their findings is having a serious effect on career outcomes for women.

So, why don't we speak up? Because we know that there's a backlash to bragging about ourselves. In another study, researchers embedded themselves within a professional development program for women at a large US organization. They found:

> The women in our study were keenly aware of the rewards of visibility. They knew that being noticed—for example, by interjecting during meetings and taking

> credit for accomplishments—was a conventional strategy for professional advancement. Still, many women consciously rejected that strategy.
>
> Instead, they opted for a risk-averse, conflict-avoidant strategy in the office. Women employed this "intentional invisibility" when they avoided conflict with colleagues, softened their assertiveness with niceness, and "got stuff done" by quietly moving things forward without drawing attention to themselves. The consequence of this approach was that they often ended up feeling well-liked but underappreciated.

These women knew that visibility would lead to career advancement, but many of them chose to remain invisible. The researchers found that the women, among other things, wanted to avoid the backlash of bragging. Many of them had either experienced or witnessed situations in which women who acted with authority or assertiveness were penalized.

Most of my clients come to me determined to help their career and learn how to promote themselves, and most of them also worry about experiencing backlash. Yes, there's a chance that you will experience backlash. Of course there is. But there's also a chance that you won't experience any negative consequences as a result of your bragging. In fact, it's far more likely that by learning to speak up for yourself (and others), you will see your career and your prospects grow by leaps and bounds.

To be perfectly clear, I'm not bothered by the idea that you might go out there and be bold, brash, aggressive, blunt, or standoffish. I'm bothered by the fact that you might avoid bragging about yourself and sharing your accomplishments because you're worried about being those things. I did not write this book to help you continue to be "nice" or to teach you to manage other people's feelings—I wrote it to teach you to Brag Better about yourself and to help other people do the same.

Are there people, particularly women, around you who speak directly? If so, study their directness. Use them as role models and reminders to yourself for how to remove verbal undercutting and clearly state your accomplishments and what you want.

When it comes to being loud, I want you to practice saying what you accomplished, saying what you mean, and saying what you want as simply and plainly as possible, with no fluff, no sugarcoating, no tiptoeing around. I'm not going to promise you that the wage gap will disappear and systemic sexism and racism in the workplace will vanish, but I believe that your work environment will change for the better when you learn to use your voice and say what you mean.

## The Brag Breakdown with Cindy Gallop: Bullshit Like a Man

*For activist Cindy Gallop, fierce voice for women and founder of MakeLoveNotPorn, bullshitting is a crucial skill. She wants every woman to learn to shoot the breeze like men, for their own gain. Here's how.*

### Self-Promotion Is a Good Thing

"I readily say to women, *Why do you say the words 'self-promotion' like it's a bad thing?* If you don't promote yourself, who the hell else is going to? . . . I want you to bullshit like men do. And I use that specific word because I feel completely confident in asking women to bullshit. It doesn't matter how much you think you're bullshitting, you will never, ever bullshit at the level that men do."

### And Bragging Is the Just Thing to Do

"When you think you're bullshitting, all you're doing is *doing justice to yourself*. And [that goes] for any woman who thinks she's bragging: all you're doing when you're bragging is doing justice to yourself."

### Brag Because the World Tells You Not to

"From the minute we're born as women we are made to feel insecure about absolutely everything to do with ourselves: the way we look, the way we talk, the way we dress. 'Nice girls do this,' 'Nice girls don't do that.' We spend the rest of our lives coming back from that and some of us never do."

### Say What You Think

"It's a single micro-action that will transform your life and your career going forward. Say what you think. No, really. Say what you *really* think. Because we don't. Especially as women. Every day we are mansplained to, manterrupted, talked over, not listened to, condescended, patronized. . . . Say what you think because, quite often, only then do you find out what you really think. If you constantly suppress your true opinion, you cease to have it and cease to own it."

### Your Voice Is Your Value

"You are hired for what you uniquely bring to the table, your unique perspectives and insights and points of view. . . . Ask for the highest amount of money you can say out loud without actually bursting out laughing. That's all you have to do. You need to project that value. Look at everything you've accomplished and own it—and ask for what you're worth."

## The Building Blocks for Your Brags

There is no such thing as the perfect brag. However, there are four elements that can make constructing a good brag easier. How you use these four elements will heavily depend on the scenario, too. Sometimes you really want to ham it up (that's me, often—in case you can't tell, I love attention). Sometimes you want to be firm, or more gracious and deferring, but it's up to you. You are in the driver's seat here.

### THE DNA OF A GREAT BRAG: GRATITUDE, PRIDE, PRESENTATION, AND SHOWMANSHIP

First and foremost, Bragging Better is the interplay of your internal dialogue, how you feel about yourself and your work, your outward performance, and how you communicate that to others. I begin my brag essentials with how you feel on the inside.

The four elements required for a good brag are gratitude, pride, presentation, and showmanship. Think of them as a rubric—you're not married to it, but you're kinda dating. They don't all have to be used every time you talk about yourself, but they are an important inflection point to think about when you do speak up. They can be used in any combination or alone.

#### *Gratitude*

It's amazing what happens when you decide to be grateful and vocalize it. I've found that when I emphasize gratitude, it engenders feelings of joy both in myself and those around me. That's a broad net to cast, but it mostly means recognizing what you've got going on and feeling groovy about it.

Be thankful when sharing about yourself. You've chosen to show up here, put your big girl (or boy, or nonconforming) pants on, and do the damn thing. Congrats! Each win—big or small—required your hard work and that of others. Step back and look at what you've accomplished to calibrate where you are and feel good about it. Gratitude can also mean saying thank you to yourself and those around you every once in a while. It can be hard to do, but it's pretty rewarding. It puts you in a positive mindset to be thankful for where you are, where you've come from, and where you're going. You might feel like you haven't "gotten" anywhere because you are inundated by the "shiny" brags posted across the internet. Guess what: there isn't really a firm arrival point for any of us, so there is no true "getting" anywhere.

Gratitude can be incredibly difficult when it feels like other people around you are succeeding more than you are. It can feel really crappy, all the time. I get it. I regularly look at someone's Instagram or new company and think he or she is just plain better than I am, or prettier, or has cuter outfits. And every time I do it, I feel worse. Practicing gratitude—being thankful and grateful for the amazing things I *do* have versus what I *don't*—might seem like an empty suggestion for making yourself feel better, but it actually works. When we live in a culture of new, now, and next, gratitude can be extremely difficult to hold on to. It's a muscle you need to train.

Gratitude takes time and practice. Search for what you're grateful for in your work. I often make a list and include everything that I'm grateful for, no matter how small a feat or characteristic it might seem. My list might include "I finished writing that article today," or "I made my bed today," or "I love my dog so much I could just explode." Whether you're grateful you got through a speech or even got through a tough meeting, little wins build up to big ones. And reflecting on that is a great practice so that you don't forget where you've come from. I need reminding of that, too.

### Claire Saffitz: The Overwhelming Feeling Is Gratitude

*Claire Saffitz didn't expect to be a viral YouTube star. The chef, host of* Bon Appétit's Gourmet Makes, *and author of an upcoming baking book was more used to cooking up a storm behind the scenes. She certainly didn't expect millions to tune in to her adventures in making junk food.*

"It was never a goal of mine to be in front of a camera. I've never thought of myself as a performer in any way. And I've never been very comfortable with the idea of people looking at me or being the center of attention. [Being on camera] has helped me to explore other parts of my personality that I have maybe underacknowledged. I've also had to confront parts of my personality that aren't well-suited to it—my intense introversion."

#### How to Counter Introversion?

"I think the overwhelming feeling is one of gratitude. I'm so grateful that people are watching the videos and enjoying them. People's feedback has helped me understand what exactly they get out of it. It's this sense of diversion that is missing from people's daily lives, and that makes me feel great."

A healthy attitude of gratitude also makes a really good practice for being conscious of what you are appreciative of in your life and what makes you feel better. A roundup of several research studies in Harvard's *Healthbeat* newsletter found that "giving thanks can make you happier." Speaking of gratitude, thank you for reading this book! I would be so grateful if you bought one for a friend. Wink, wink.

Here are some suggested words and phrasing for showing gratitude when sharing a brag:

- I'm so thrilled and grateful that my idea made it into the main project presentation. It looks great. How can I make sure that happens again?
- I loved working with this client, and I think he liked my work, too. I was so thankful for that opportunity. I'd love to have a chance to lead a project with a similar client.
- Thank you so much for singing my praises in that meeting. It made me feel good and that my work matters.
- I am so thankful to share the video from a panel I participated in.
- I'm honored to be a part of this list of executives in my industry.
- Thank you so much for featuring me. And on your cover, no less! If the twelve-year-old me knew this, she'd be freaking out right now.
- Can't believe I get to be in this room of amazing women. I'm so grateful.

Make sure that the language you use matches what you use in regular conversation. If your coworkers regularly hear you say that you are honored, thankful, and fortunate in relation to non-brags, then this phrasing will sound authentic. If those around you only associate this language with your brags, you will sound disingenuous.

Sharing feelings of gratitude helps spread positive feelings. When you include the people who were involved in your accomplishments, it helps to create supportive environments going forward. When you share gratitude, you undercut any icky feelings around bragging. If you say something like, "I feel so lucky to have been a part of this special project" or "I feel endlessly grateful to have been given the chance to lead the growth in my division," your emotion helps people connect to your accomplishments, and those warm fuzzies make them want to work with you more. It also simply feels nice.

### *Pride*

You should be proud of the work you've done and communicate that to others. "Should" is a tough word, and we usually use it in the context of judging ourselves for something we haven't done. In this case, I'm trying to tell you that your ideas and work *are* worthy of praise and visibility. But accepting that is super difficult. Part of Bragging Better is accepting that you deserve praise, and then figuring out what to do with that praise. When you're conditioned to feel constantly critical of yourself, expressing pride can feel rotten and you might feel undeserving. It takes a lot of thought and getting behind yourself and your work. I am working on this all the time, too, as my instinct is to speak poorly to myself and be hypercritical.

Being proud is important, but it can feel counterintuitive. We are so quick to put ourselves down. "When somebody says something that you did sucked, you might think, 'You're right,'" says Luvvie Ajayi. And yet, "When people say something that you did was amazing, you doubt them. How is it that we accept criticism, but we don't accept praise?"

Part of the beauty of pride is getting to lead by example, and it's a liberating example. By sharing this sentiment, you encourage the people reading or hearing your bragging to feel pride in their accomplishments as well. You've done the work, you're sharing facts, and you can be proud of it. You have to lead the pride conga line, and I think you might find that once you start doing it, others will follow.

As Kimberly Drew, social media strategist, art historian, and art critic, points out, "There are so many of us [especially women of color] who have been intimidated out of trusting ourselves because of media controls, because of really toxic work environments. We hear, 'Oh, you're so arrogant,' 'You're so bigheaded,' 'You're so self-absorbed.' But who else are you going to absorb? Why not absorb yourself? Why not celebrate yourself? The world would rather that we not exist in some spaces—why would you not just flex harder?" This also helps others Brag Better, too. Seeing you brag might help someone else share something he or she would never have shared previously, so set a good example.

Try these suggested or example words and phrasing:

- So proud of this report I wrote last week.
- Delighted that I was included in this panel among other movers and shakers in the business.
- I'm so proud of this big project I turned in on time, and it did well for one of our biggest accounts.

### *Presentation*

Gratitude and pride are internal attitudes, and cultivating them allows you to show up for yourself fully. Presentation links to the tailoring of your brag for the audience you want to reach. Knowing how to Brag Better requires that you be intentional about how your present your accomplishments—you're not just stating them. If you bungle the display, or fail to consider the medium you're working with, it can fall flat—and then it doesn't work and you've potentially wasted a great outfit (my personal fear).

Consider how your brags are displayed. Think about your audience and what they would appreciate. Decide on the best delivery method. Will you brag verbally, via email, on social media, in a meeting, or in a speech? A combination?

Presentation should vary from audience to audience and application to application. For example, when sharing a brag on a platform like Instagram, it should be a clear, demonstrative photo-based brag, and one with hashtags and links to other handles, as well as a driver to a link in your bio. Always consider the presentation of what you're sharing and the context in which it is being shared.

Share your brag in a way that is unique to you. Don't run yourself ragged trying to be someone that you're not. Don't take yourself too seriously, but present in a way that feels authentic, real, and honest. Use words that are comfortable for you, and don't be afraid to take up some space.

Use these suggested or example words and phrasing:

- Thrilled to share this photo from my speech. You can watch video of it in the link in my bio. Thank you to the hosts @host and @otherpanelists. (Instagram)
- I wanted to share an article I wrote. Please help me amplify it: "I loved @yourhandle's article. Read more at (link)." (Twitter)

## The Brag Breakdown with Emma Gray: Stand in Your Space

*For author and host Emma Gray, deciding to stand in your message is difficult. Yet the mind behind* A Girl's Guide to Joining the Resistance *has managed to stay grounded and pay it forward. Here's how she does it.*

### Standing in Your Space Doesn't Require a Grand Gesture

"If you want to be a podcaster, record a podcast episode. Record a pilot on your laptop. If you want to write, write for yourself. Just move that muscle. Open yourself up to both the disappointment of rejection and excitement of validation because both of those things are just an integral part of any career.

"Women are socialized to be nurturers. Bragging, or just owning your accomplishments, involves taking up more space, asserting to the world that you did something that is of value and deserves to be both a physical and mental presence."

### Talk About Your Work

"[So many] women who have been conditioned to take up less space can have a hard time owning our accomplishments. . . . [I've caught] myself writing bios for myself and forgetting to mention that I wrote a book. I [also] have to really check myself when people say, 'Congratulations, you wrote a book.' I'll say, 'Oh, that was a year ago. It's a super small book. It wasn't a best-seller.' I'll find myself cutting down my accomplishments, whereas the people talking to me don't care about those numbers, don't care about the ways in which I feel like I failed or [that] the person sitting next to me has done the thing I've done better."

**Your Friends Are Your Best Hype**

"My best friends are my best viral marketers. It's much harder to do that for yourself. A good exercise is [to ask], 'What would my very best friend in the world say about me? What would he or she say they love about me?' Then you need to talk about yourself like that—with all of the love, care, and affection of a close friend."

**Progress Will Take Time**

"It's all of these screwed-up gender norms that create a situation where women feel unequal or feel like they don't have the space to sell themselves in a way that won't reflect poorly on them. I don't want to minimize the very real kind of dance that women, people of color, and queer people have to do on a daily basis to navigate that personal empowerment. . . . [But] my optimism is bolstered when I see these more massive shifts. When I see more women in positions of power, in Congress, or in newsrooms. I think the systems will hopefully eventually shift, but we have a long way to go."

### *Showmanship*

You've nailed the content, tone, and delivery, and now it's all about pizzazz. Showmanship is the icing and flair on top of presentation. It's letting your personality shine, a little "zhuhzing" up, if you will. I, of course, like putting on a show. It's time for you to put on a show for yourself, in a way that feels true to you.

You can have a little fun, too. Bragging Better doesn't require that you be so serious. Work hard but then toss in a little confetti along the way. Be prepared, but let that preparation give you the space for some fun. By having the basics down pat, you can play around and tinker with what you're sharing, see what feels good and fun, and iterate from there.

Your sense of humor matters, so don't be afraid to punch it up a little. A survey by the employment tech firm Robert Half found that "roughly four in five (79 percent) CFOs said an employee's sense of humor plays an important role in how well he or she fits in with the company's corporate culture." Humor is important for leaders, too. The Bell Leadership Institute surveyed 2,700 workers and found that, when describing the strengths of leaders within their organizations, the phrases "sense of humor" and "work ethic" were by far the most frequent.

Being funny and brazen can get you the gig, too. A CareerBuilder survey of over two thousand hiring managers found that, if presented with two equally qualified job candidates, a sense of humor was the most-cited factor that managers used to consider one candidate over the other. By adding your own unique spin and being able to poke fun at yourself (without verbal undercutting), you are showing people your personality. Your personality and how you share it is a huge part of doing the bragging work. Someone once called me the "Jimmy Kimmel of women's entrepreneurship," and let me tell you, I am still running with that.

The more fun you're having, the more others will want to join in and feel that fun, too. When I first started speaking, I was so intent on "nailing" everything that I forgot to have fun. It took time and space for me to be able to have fun onstage, and I also watched a lot of stand-up comedians I admire. I added some physical humor and some things that made me laugh.

Humor will help you engage with an audience, but also remember that the point of this is to get to a place where you feel good and have a good time. If humor or wackiness is a part of who you are and who you want to share with the universe, go for it. This is particularly true if you're in comedy or acting, but it's also true if it's simply a part of your personality that you want to bring into your professional world every day. Showing who you are only humanizes you.

I love memes, and I am a self-proclaimed comedy nerd. For a long time I didn't think I could incorporate them into who I was as a professional. I had to be a serious businessperson! I couldn't be funny. Then I realized I was missing a huge part of my personality. For ages, the FinePoint website and my materials, including my personal site, were boring and presented an image that I thought made me worthy of hiring.

People aren't hiring a website; they're hiring *you*. It wasn't until I got more comfortable with people hiring me for me, and not what I thought a businessperson looked like, that I realized sanitizing myself and my materials was holding people back from hiring me instead of incentivizing them to do so. I now add humor and color to everything that I do.

Showmanship can be really personal, and it varies from bragger to bragger. Showmanship means showcasing what you've done in a way that feels true and fun to you. While it takes experimentation and learning, sometimes that means trying out a particular phrase you like to use, or showcasing a skill in a new way. For example, I had a friend share a series of highlights of her speaking, but she presented it in a cool collage, which allowed her to use her artistic flair. She was able to show two parts of herself, incorporate a memorable brag, and do it in a way that was true to her. When you do this for yourself, you could use other personal flair, like adding a GIF or video clip, making your sentences rhyme (sometimes cheesy but also cute!), or trying out a pun.

## What Comes First Matters

The focus of being loud isn't only volume—you must also pay attention to the order in which you choose your words. The descriptors you use are important, but what you say first matters the most. We remember what we hear first. When I lived in Los Angeles, I was always tickled by how everyone I encountered would introduce themselves by their aspirations. I met a lot of actors, music producers, and musicians who were also my Uber drivers.

This, among others, is one reason why I tell people that the order of their descriptors can help determine and drive where they want to go. For example, I had a client named Sara, who worked for the government as an investigator for her agency (that sounds like spy-speak, but she wasn't a spy).

Sure, Sara enjoyed what she did, but she wanted to mediate more and investigate less—she wanted to help parties negotiate a settlement. I told her she had to start referring to herself as a mediator or she wouldn't get to where she wanted to go. She wouldn't be lying. Sara had mediated before. But she had to hype that part of her skill set because it was what she wanted to do more of in the future. The more she told people that she was an investigator first, the more she would get asked to do that kind of work and be known as an investigator.

For Sara, it felt unnatural to claim a title that she feared she had barely earned. But it was only *her* idea of having "earned it"—I reminded her that so many of us feel like we have to have a doctorate to feel we've earned a certain title. Remember my music producer Uber drivers? They had dreams and didn't want to be defined by driving me to LAX.

Sara began to use the term "mediator" first when describing

what she did. As a result, her boss noticed. She changed her social media and bios to list mediator at the beginning instead of at the end. Her boss saw that she had placed the emphasis on the mediator title, which made her take Sara more seriously as a mediator. In conversations with attorneys, they noted her interest and began to ask for her by name. More opportunities came her way through management—opportunities to attend more training and mediate more cases, which gave her the experience she craved. Eventually, she was tasked with training the other mediators in her agency as the team grew. It was her adoption of the title "mediator" that helped other people in her agency to see her as a mediator.

I see this mistake all the time—my clients will want to be recognized for one aspect of their career, but they put that description of themselves at the very end of their bios. Then they get frustrated because they're not recognized for the aspect they most want to develop. I had one client who wanted to get more speaking gigs and felt dismayed by the lack of response she was getting. In all of her bios, she listed herself as a writer, philanthropist, and speaker. "Speaker" was last in her description of herself, and the emphasis was elsewhere. It was no surprise that people took her more seriously as a writer than they did as a speaker.

This is incredibly common. We describe ourselves as we know ourselves to be, not in terms of what we want to be. My client wanted to become a speaker, but she knew herself as a writer. I coached her to begin using the word "speaker" first in her descriptions of herself—in all of her bios, on her résumé, on her website, in her email signatures. Once she began to describe herself in goal-oriented terms, she began to book speaking gigs.

Your description of yourself needs to be goal-oriented,

instead of a list of things you do in order from best to most speculative. You're in charge of how people see you.

## Sharing and Vulnerability

Being vulnerable, whether it's with personal health struggles, mental health, or everyday difficulties, is also important. Nobody wants to see a pristine robot that's not relatable or truthful. The more you open up to a degree that feels comfortable to you, the better.

It's a tough line to walk, I will admit. But vulnerability and honesty are important for feeling aligned with your true self, and these qualities also help other people see the real you. A particularly low point in 2015 made that clear to me. A big project of mine, one I had pinned my hopes and dreams on (I had poorly set expectations), had crumbled. I was crushed. I was confused, anxious, and sad (extremely depressed, as someone who struggles with both depression and anxiety and gets help for it can say). I decided to spill my guts to a Listserv of powerful and thoughtful women, asking for help, reassurance, and guidance. It wasn't full-on public, but I was broadcasting these sentiments far and wide. I was terrified to hit "send."

As a result, I got over one hundred responses. Women I didn't know called to ask how I was and to talk through things. Women I had never met sent me cards and gifts, told me they were "going through it, too," and, suddenly, I felt less alone. I felt supported, not to mention shocked. I wish it hadn't taken me feeling so low to reach out and ask for help, but it did teach me the power of honesty and vulnerability. Years later, it's still mentioned to me by women in that group. My share made a lasting impression, but not in the sense that it made me seem like a weakling. It was appreciated. I won't ever forget that power, even when I felt so hopeless. The response was a tremendous display of kindness and empathy.

Not everyone will be comfortable with you showing your true self. Someone else from that Listserv sat me down a few years later at a dinner and told me I shouldn't have sent that email. She said that it made me look "weak" to potential clients. It showed how uncomfortable she was sharing her truth with others, and it wasn't in line with the overall response I got. I was furious at her not only for thinking it was okay to say that to me, but also for projecting her own vulnerability issues onto me. Showmanship matters, but not just around your wins. Sometimes what you think makes you feel "weak" is actually the most powerful of all.

## Make Bragging Regularly a Habit

So much of Bragging Better is simply being prepared—making yourself think of and prepare for scenarios in which you may have an opportunity to share your thoughts, voice your accomplishments, or speak an unpopular opinion. It's a good idea to think of bragging as a habit, like brushing your teeth, and to do it regularly. Here are a few ideas:

- Put it in your calendar and brag on a weekly or monthly basis.
- Track your accomplishments and the benchmarks you've reached throughout the year so that you are prepared to share these facts with your boss or manager.
- Make sure that at least once a month you are including brags in your email communication to your manager and to those you report to.

- Share your smaller accomplishments on a weekly basis so that those around you can track your continued progress.
- List examples of where to look for brags in your life so that you are ready to record them when they happen.
- Consider awards, promotions, or growth of any kind inside the office.
- Brag about accomplishments outside of the office related to your volunteer efforts, sports teams, or community work.

Consider the natural moments where a brag will feel organic. Sometimes it might not, and you have to force yourself to do it anyway. Is there a point in each weekly meeting when you are asked to share your wins? If so, be prepared with a crafted response. If there isn't, you're going to have to prompt yourself and lead by example. You could even make it a practice, so that everyone around you has the ability to share their wins, too.

What are some of the most important moments to brag about that you regularly forget? Make sure that you are ready with a brag if you are asked to share. And don't let an opportunity pass where you can brag on behalf of your team.

## Ready, Set, Go!

▶ **Craft several brags using the four key elements that make up a brag: gratitude, pride, presentation, and showmanship.**

# 5

# Be Strategic

I once counseled a group of executives on their personal brands and voices, and then I was asked to counsel the younger members of the organization—some of whom were straight out of college. One junior employee in particular was the youngest hire, and she had a long way to go in making herself heard. All she wanted was to be able to speak up and be listened to in meetings.

This was made a little harder due to the fact that her boss was one of the most magnetic, visible, and successful women in the company, one who had no trouble being outspoken. This senior woman couldn't understand why the junior associate couldn't simply speak up more. She tried to encourage her to do so, but their styles were so different.

I completely understood the younger woman's hesitation. She enjoyed listening and was a keen member of The Qualified Quiet who wanted to absorb all the information before making a calculated response.

The junior employee and I met several times to discuss a strategy to get her to speak up in meetings and, eventually, to speak up with clients and colleagues. We began small. I challenged her to ask a question in one meeting each week. We went over all the details, including where she would sit, and scripted out exactly what she would say. I had her speak to a mentor at the company and ask them to help echo her voice and empower her to feel okay speaking up to the rest of the group. She went in each week with a piece of paper with at least one question written on it. Many people wonder about the image of bringing notes into a meeting with them. I tell them to do it—if anything, you only look more prepared. Nobody knows what's on that slip of paper. Preparedness assuages so many Bragging Better fears.

Over time, she asked one question a week, and bit by bit, it started to feel easier to do. Eventually, she didn't need the slip of paper or the calculated decisions about where to sit—she was comfortable enough contributing that she no longer needed to make such detailed plans. By the time our work together ended, she was consistently contributing in meetings and in conversations with colleagues.

Having a strategy for your brags includes being clear on what you want, knowing your audience, and doing the prep work to get it.

What is *your* dream signal of visibility—your dream result of Bragging Better?

Maybe it's a prestigious internship. A great first job. Feeling better while networking, which is the world's most boring sport (but an important one). Maybe you want to win a board seat, earn a giant raise (get that money, honey!), or take your company public.

This is something I ask every prospective client, every friend, and every colleague that I want to see succeed. I have them state out loud what their dream, pie-in-the-sky, no-holds-barred brag would look like. For me, my ultimate brag will have been achieved when I am on the cover of *Vogue*, in a couture ball gown, languishing over a fainting couch while my dog looks on in admiration (I have never thought about this, clearly). Often, that dream brag is a classic one, like an op-ed in the *New York Times*.

It doesn't have to be a huge win, either. You can start small, like that junior associate did—all she wanted as her initial goal was to be able to speak up and contribute in meetings. Your dream brag might involve getting the big promotion you've been working toward or getting a bonus for closing the most sales in a year. Your dream bit of visibility can also be a speaking gig way above your normal fee. A good friend was in a bad mood when she got asked for a quote for a potential speaking gig, and she added an extra zero to her number just for fun. They said yes. Shoot for the moon, and you could end up in a pile of cash.

Let yourself go there, imagine, and dream. It's fun, but it's also very telling. Sometimes your dream brag isn't exactly in your field, but you love *Rolling Stone* so much you just want to be on that cover, strumming a guitar you don't know how to play. Never say never. And you'd be surprised what happens once you name what you want. Then you have something to work toward.

## What Do You Want?

This can be a very scary question, and one that can be broken down and tailored precisely to you. It's scary because it's almost too big to answer, and it changes throughout our lives. It's hard to answer something so important, so a lot of us avoid getting clear on it in the first place.

The answer differs for everyone, at each point in your life, throughout your career. Drill down on what you want from Bragging Better. Get out a pen and paper and write down exactly what you want to achieve—this week, this month, and this year. Breaking it down makes it a lot less scary.

Now consider what each of the goals or wants listed means to you.

- A pay raise leads to more money for vacations with your friends or family.
- More time to speak in a meeting means a greater ability to contribute.
- Being published feels like your thoughts are being heard.
- A promotion results in having your colleagues look to you more often.
- Getting that extra-zero speaking gig leads to bigger and better gigs.

Figuring out what you want is daunting, but it will help serve as the beginning of your road map. I'll use myself as an example. As I said, I want to be on the cover of *Vogue*. (I'm hoping if I loudly state my specific desire in my book, it will manifest itself. Call me, *Vogue*.)

## Why Do You Want It?

Now, why do you want that? Is it because it will make you feel like a more treasured employee? Is it for clout? Is it because you know you deserve it but are afraid to ask? Is it because you *just want to*, which is a perfectly good answer? The why helps put the want into action. Sit for a minute with these ideas and decide your why. Your why doesn't have to be grand or astronomical; it simply has to be a guiding light for what you desire. I want to be in *Vogue* because I love fashion, and I can think of nothing more glamorous than being in *Vogue* as confirmation of my status as a style icon (in my head at least).

## How Do You Think You'll Get It?

There are numerous ways to achieve your goals, but you want to know how being proud, loud, and strategic will get you there and why. Look at your Brag Better goals for this week and this month, and think about the steps you need to take to achieve them (those for the year are harder to answer). There are several ways to get something, so consider the path, too.

Back to *Vogue*—I'll take a look at the kind of authors or entrepreneurs they write about. Do I know anyone working there? Can I sniff around to find the right person to pitch? Can I come up with a pitch that would be compelling for the editors at *Vogue*?

## What Do You Want to Be Known for?

The question of what you want to be known for is big, scary, and overwhelming. This question is challenging for me, and I do this *for a living*. We all contain multitudes, and it can feel very hard to nail down some specific answers here. That's okay. It's important that we make an attempt to figure out what we truly want so we can strategize appropriately, even if it feels hard.

This is a question you are going to contend with in varying forms for most of your career and your life. Don't feel that you must have the perfect answer right away. You shouldn't. Let's talk about the next, say, two to four years. Let's talk about next month. Next week. What are you doing tomorrow? I always tell people that they can wear many hats, but they can only wear one hat outside until pretty soon they are known for their ugly fedora (or whichever hat type you choose). In order to stick out in someone's mind, you have to know what you want him or her to see. This isn't set in stone, but if you're able to answer this question, even if it's vague at first, it will help set you up for success.

This question will also change over time. As you grow up, your desires will change alongside your age. You'll pursue other facets of your career, or even industries, and your answers will change.

If you're having trouble answering this question, you're not alone. Consider asking a few varied people in your orbit what they think you are currently known for. You might also ask them what they think you *should* be known for. Their answers can help you focus or realign if they are very different from how you'd like to be perceived.

You could send a survey to a group of people in your circle. What's important about this list of people is that each sees you from a different angle. Pick a family member, a close friend, someone you're friendly with, a coworker, someone you've worked with in the past, and maybe someone you know only over social media. Then email them one or more of the following questions, asking for their help and explaining some context:

- What do you think I do?
- How would you explain my job?
- What would you tell someone else about my career and work?

These answers will help you figure out if what you're putting out is in line with what you think about yourself and what you want. It also brings other people into your journey. They are resources, and it helps them think about their messages, too. A family member loves you but might not properly understand what you do. A close friend might see you as a friend and not a professional. A social media acquaintance can give you perspective on how to talk to the world at large. Our connections can be a great mirror, holding up a picture of you to make sure it aligns with the one you want.

Being "known" also means something different to everyone. It doesn't mean being on a magazine cover on a fainting couch in a ball gown exclusively. You could be known in your community, in your larger social circle, or within your company.

Being "known" doesn't require that you find your exact "lane"—that can take years, if not decades. Instead, focus more on finding a large open road where you can start to walk.

Part of this question is to encourage my clients away from big-picture terms like "visionary," "disruptor," or "thought leader." You cannot be known for a super general, fluid term right off the bat. Those titles mean something different to everyone. The second someone comes to me and tells me they want to be known as an "influencer" before anything else, my eyes roll into the back of my head and then we get to work crafting a succinct narrative grounded in reality.

This can play out across your industry. For example, when you see a general commentator, he or she never got there as a generalist to begin with. I have a friend who was known as an expert on a hyper-specific women's issue. She went on TV, did very well, and commented on more women's issues, then broader political issues, and now almost any issue. You have to slam-dunk one topic first before you play all the positions (I do not think I did that sports analogy correctly, but you get the gist).

Let's go back to Nina. Nina killed her first TV appearance, which was on a hyper-specific political issue. Later she was interviewed again on that same issue, but then, since she was good in the medium, quick on her feet, and knew her stuff, she was booked again to discuss an adjacent political issue. She now comments across political issues, on broad questions about our political system, political parties, and political elections. She started small and moved outward.

Your "lane" or key subject matter should be something you truly care about. The examples I use of television appearances and books seem like peak accomplishments, but they serve to show you that passion wins on the big stage, and it also wins on a smaller one. In fact, it has to win on the small stage first before you take it to the main arena. If you love your work, care about what you do, and begin to share that, it will resonate.

Some people want to be known for whatever will get them known fastest, and that might work for a short period of time, but it never has lasting power. Ask anyone who has been called an "overnight success"—there is no such thing. And if there is, you need the skills to carry out a longer-term vision to sustain that status. I want to know what's in your heart, and I want you to share *that*.

## Considering Your Audience

Everyone's audience is different, and bragging to the audience you want to market to, sell to, or influence is key. It can take trial and error to figure out where exactly your peeps are, but the first step is to start from your goals and work from there.

I had a client, let's call her Leah, who was looking to sell her company. Leah was in the education technology sector, a fast-growing industry and one that has a lot of players. She wanted to sell her already successful company to a larger entity so that it could grow and flourish with more resources. However, she was bragging in a way that wasn't helping her with that goal. She was raising her profile to others in the industry and to other entrepreneurs, but that was not where her potential buyers were. In other words, she was focusing on the wrong audience. Part of Bragging Better is understanding where your audience is, what they are reading, and what they in particular want to see in order for you to get what you want. In this case, she was not doing those things.

Sure, Leah was talking about how her inspiring and thoughtful programming was great. However, what she was truly looking for was for a large company to buy her out. We had to talk differently to a new audience, which meant we needed to cater to what those big cheeses cared about. We started promoting Leah's company in a way that touted what these companies cared about (success in terms of growth, management, and profits), in a way they would understand ($$$), and in the places they respected (outlets that covered acquisitions, deals, and investors). We strategized around the five companies that were her ideal buyers. What were they reading? Where were they consuming information? What past companies had they purchased?

Because we were clear on which audience she wanted to reach and how to reach them, we were able to target Leah's audience effectively. We bragged about her company and leadership in a way that was appealing to that audience.

Not only did we need to go where they were, but we also needed to speak their language. Though Leah wasn't in finance, she had to get down to the nitty-gritty and discuss the numbers when bragging about her company. How quickly she had grown, how much money she was pulling in, and their projected profits were all key. That is what a company cares about when acquiring a business. Yes, the content and heart matters, but if it's an investment, it's money that really talks.

This helped Leah focus her desires. She stopped bragging in the way she had before—to others who already knew how great she was or to her immediate audience. She changed her tone and what she was touting. And by doing that, she had the right material to show for an acquisition meeting. We prominently featured her company's revenue and other indicators of performance and value. Had she only worked on getting general attention, it wouldn't have reinforced her goal. Anyone can get attention. But attention toward your professional goals is the point here.

Arguably just as important as *who* your audience is, is *where* they exist and live, either online or offline. This could mean but isn't limited to video, television, print magazines, online outlets, podcasts, and more. If your audience listens to podcasts, doing a TED Talk isn't going to get you in front of them.

We live in lots of different spaces, everyone consuming content or getting an understanding from different angles. Not only are we in different spaces—I'm scrolling Instagram a lot, I'll admit—but also we are consuming at different times of day and in different ways. I like to give myself a certain amount of time on Instagram, in the morning and at night. Timing matters, too. I also send a company newsletter based on "optimal" timing for my audience, something that is easily calculated (well, an algorithm calculates it for me).

Not only is constructing a solid brag important, but so is your timing in deploying it. Jesse came to me with a conundrum: She wanted to make the case for getting more assistance in her current role. She felt too bogged down and knew the company needed to hire someone to help her with her workload. However, she was in a classic bind a lot of women and capable people face—asking for help without being labeled "weak." Jesse was afraid of giving the impression that she couldn't handle her business.

We came up with a game plan to create brags that projected strength while also communicating a deep need. I had Jesse start bragging regularly to her boss about all the work she did. She would end her brags by sharing what more she could do if she had more time. Her boss already knew she was a valuable asset to the team, but hadn't seen how her time could be used even more effectively. We timed the touting of her wins to when she knew that her boss was going into budgeting meetings, which meant that the topic of funds for hiring for the next year would be front and center. Her framing of the issue and the timing in bringing it up led to an ultimate win for everyone. Jesse's boss used a recruiter to help Jesse find the coworker she desperately needed.

Timing right might mean a different medium based on your message, like video, or one that fits your industry, like meeting in person. More traditional industries do better with the messaging and mediums that are the norm. If you're in law, writing for a review or an industry outlet is going to make a lot more sense than posting videos on YouTube. Consider the message but also very much the medium. You might even have multiple audiences, so consider them all.

## Who Are You Bragging to (and for)?

Bragging Better isn't shouting into the abyss, it's having a direct aim and firing. Who, and sometimes more importantly where, is your audience? Each audience differs significantly. It's hard to realize and understand that each time you post, speak, or write, the audience is slightly or majorly different. No two audiences are the same in content or appearance. Which means that each time you brag, you have an opportunity to win more fans, but you also have the chance to practice your bragging and tailor it specifically to an audience.

While some of The Qualified Quiet are aiming at public-facing brags and audiences, it's also important to know your audience at work, which is important to the livelihood of your job, your coworkers, and those you work for.

Your everyday brags with your boss and colleagues are about small wins and what it means for your team and for you. This isn't about sharing credit when you did all the work; rather, it's about creating a long-term, consistent strategy for Bragging Better with those you work with every day. Sometimes it's just as important to highlight your team. Some of walking that line will have to be evaluated by screwing it up.

I lasted about five months working for someone else, and in that time, I managed to brag pretty poorly. I wasn't into my job and I made my disinterest clear, which in retrospect was embarrassing. I wasn't considering my audience, either; I would go over the heads of many midrange managers because I knew some of the C-suite. I also put my feet on my desk. Yikes. Don't do any of that. Basically, I acted like a brat.

Consider the hierarchy in which you work and use that to your advantage. Begin with a few brags each week, testing them out among colleagues or someone you're close to, and then with those more senior than you are. They can be super small. Maybe you contributed to a project and it went over really well with a client. Maybe you had a tough but necessary conversation with a colleague. Start by recognizing what you've done and what needs to be shared so that you can advance and be a better team member, then move outward from there.

## BRAGGING TO YOUR BOSS

Bragging Better in front of your boss is tricky. Your boss is a necessary person to impress, and one that gives a lot of us a headache. So how do you showcase what you've done to your boss without it being uncomfortable while also benefiting you both?

Everyone has a different metric of success and wants to be bragged to differently. It's important to be speaking the same bragging language. For example, if your boss cares about seeing numbers, constantly talking about how comfortable you made a client, while it is a success to you, might not be a success to her. You can have this discussion openly, too. You can always ask someone how he or she would like to see the wins—whether it's in person or over email, and what format works for them. You want to speak their language of success. Sometimes it's a quick meeting where you highlight your wins or a monthly rundown document.

Your managers should know when you hit your goals and when you exceed them, too. You should also get used to telling your manager your wins that they might not see or notice. Assume they're busy with their own workload, and you have to point out when you've done something great. You can also temper your brags with an understanding of what your bosses or higher-ups like to see. There's what you want to brag about, but there's also what your boss can hear or wants to hear. If your manager really likes to see a certain kind of client email as a win, be sure to emphasize when you get those. If your boss is really big on numbers, show the numbers. You want to Brag Better but also in a way that gets heard and noticed.

All of these places to Brag Better span time, money, and power. While you might feel that some are for now, and some are for the future, they're all similar—asking for what you want, showing a degree of vulnerability, and taking chances for success.

## BRAGGING TO YOUR COLLEAGUES VERSUS THE PUBLIC

Bragging to your colleagues differs from bragging to a public audience. The biggest difference is that your colleagues already know you. They know what you're about, possibly what you bring for lunch (and how it smells when you leave it in the microwave), and if they work directly with you, what you do all day, every day. The key to bragging to your colleagues is to show them the value they might not see in your job. Sure, they might know that you are managing a team that is working on graphic design, but there are a few things they don't know. They may not know exactly what managing the team entails. Who are you emailing? Whose designs are you approving? Getting into the nitty-gritty with your colleagues means that they will better understand and be able to appreciate your work product.

Your colleagues may not know the extent of your skills. Jobs are meant to have a certain description and range of activities, but sometimes you bring more to the table than what meets the eye or is in a description. If there are areas where you can provide value that aren't in the list of your current responsibilities, make them known. However, make them known as they relate to the work you can do to help others on your team, expand your workload, and show others how capable you are.

Overall, when you consider your colleagues, you need to determine your goal. Do you want them to listen to you more in meetings, pay attention to your project contributions, or let you lead more? Make a list of what you want as a result of brags to your colleagues. Moving backward from what you want, tailor a brag emphasizing how well you do what you want to be known for.

Let's say you want to have your opinions listened to in meetings. You could say something like, "I really love contributing during meetings . . . are you open to hearing from me more often?" If you're angling to do more presentations in front of a client, you could say something like, "I felt so powerful giving that speech to our new client. Can I be considered for future opportunities like that?"

## BRAGGING IN EVERYDAY OFFICE LIFE

Your coworkers, direct reports, or bosses likely see you every day. Many clients I see, those in larger organizations, fail to Brag Better because they have trouble discerning the right place and time.

Here are a few effective or appropriate times to Brag Better in everyday office life:

- In any form of review with those higher up.
- When gunning for a promotion.
- Going after an award.

- In a presentation, while tempering the work of others and acknowledging it.
- At the end of a tough workweek, when you're especially proud.
- When someone might not know or fully understand what you do.
- When someone on your team encourages you to do so (and after you sniff it out, too).

Taking cues from those around you will be important in Bragging Better in everyday office life. It can be hard to manage, but once you hit a rhythm, you can set goals for yourself, like making a key brag once a week.

## OTHER EVERYDAY BRAGS AND ETIQUETTE

Here are a few scenarios where you can Brag Better:

- **An elevator flyby:** Keep it short and sweet. Two sentences on what you're working on, why it's of interest to that person, and how you're killing it.
- **A big meeting:** Know when it's your turn to talk and take about a minute to describe what you're doing that is great and of interest to the rest of the team.
- **In an email:** Three sentences on what you're excited about in an outcome of yours, plus a compliment to another team member, plus an actionable item.
- **One-on-one:** This depends on what kind of time you have. Be sure not to run over, and have a list of three key points you want to make with that person.
- **Forwarding emails:** As long as there aren't rules about privacy, sharing a flattering email and flagging it helps you to show, not tell.

## WHAT TO DO IF YOU FEEL NERVOUS ABOUT BRAGGING INSIDE THE OFFICE

Bragging inside the office might feel unnatural to you, and you might be nervous about pulling it off. Set yourself up for success by remembering that you are just stating facts about your accomplishments and that your accomplishments are enough and worth sharing.

You're also existing in an ecosystem, and each office environment varies from workplace to workplace, within divisions, and within pods. There are a lot of office politics, and you will have to learn by trial and error about the reactions of those around you when you choose to Brag Better.

I have conversations constantly with friends and clients who ask me whether a colleague's poor reaction to their brag is their issue to deal with. First, I always want to remind people that you're not responsible for someone else's feelings. You need to "keep your side of the street clean," says a good friend of mine. But as long as you do what you believe is right, do good work, and show up proud of it, that's truly all you can do. When you're "in it" with another coworker, maybe one who is jealous or who doesn't know how to deal with your self-promotion, it can feel like it's all your fault. It's important to delineate when something is a "you" problem or a "them" problem.

I'll give you an example. I was working with a client, I'll call her Sam, who works for a giant company with a well-known name. Said giant business doesn't like it when people "brag," or so Sam thought. She was so busy tiptoeing around her boss's potential feelings (without addressing them head-on) that it ended up affecting her job. She wasn't able to properly brag in meetings, which ended up doing her, and ultimately her boss, a disservice when she didn't speak up in a key meeting where her decades of experience was very relevant. It would have immediately put her company in the position of the obvious first choice for the potential client. Instead she demurred, and they didn't get the gig. One of the first things I asked her when she presented me with this problem was, "Isn't this *his* problem?" We deduced that it was, and while she couldn't control her boss's feelings, she had to do her job.

If you're dealing with someone in your office who struggles with you Bragging Better about your work, consider ways to share the spotlight:

- Tie your brag to your department's accomplishments, making sure to brag about the contributions of the people you work with.
- Brag on behalf of someone else on your team.
- Share your excitement about accomplishing a team goal with your team and with the other stakeholders in your company.

While I recommend using any of the above tactics to help your colleagues see the benefits of bragging, I want you to remember that it isn't your responsibility to manage anyone else's feelings. Keep bragging and sharing your pride in your work, even if it ruffles some feathers. You could consider sharing brags like:

- I made a killer pitch to the higher-ups today. Want to hear it?
- I'm really proud of what I shared in that meeting just now. What did you think of it?
- Did you see that PowerPoint I shared with the group? I'm really proud of it.

. . .

I HAD A client named Claire who was brand-new at a buzzy startup. She was thrilled she snagged the job but self-conscious of her young age. For many men in the world of technology and startups, being young is seen as an asset. For women, it's much more complicated (something I desperately hope changes). To boot, the startup had just hired a slew of seasoned vets with decades of experience, making Claire feel even more intimidated. To begin with, we reframed her mindset. I told her that these industry vets were probably just as nervous over the possibility that someone younger would undercut them in an industry that unfairly values youth. I told her to assert her strengths with her coworkers. She had led impressive student organizations at school, and she needed to talk about them, even if she thought those accomplishments sounded "young," which was more a judgment of hers than the reality. I told her to talk about them—she was hired for a reason. We often bury things we think are too "junior" when they in fact tell a compelling story when timed and communicated well. Everyone has unique strengths that can help in any workplace, and Claire soon began to feel more at ease as she heard herself underscoring her sizable accomplishments. As you're practicing bragging, you might mistakenly go a bit overboard. It's up to you to find a line you can toe that works for you. If a colleague or manager expresses that they are offended by one of your brags, it's certainly good for you to take what they say into consideration. I'm not telling you to apologize for Bragging Better. What I'm telling you is to hear them out, determine if their concern is reasonable, and if it is, temper your brags in the future. Again, you will have to determine whether or not it's a "them" problem. Then it's a matter of deciding whether or not you want to change that behavior, and if that person's offense will affect your job and your ability to work.

If it is a "you" problem, then you apologize and move on. I remember doing this with an editor once. I was trying to be snarky, but instead it came out as sort of an insult. I could sense that she was upset, and although it was not my job to figure that out (I strongly believe that someone needs to tell you when they are upset—you are not a mind reader), I apologized. If you feel that you have overstepped, take the time to craft a wholehearted apology if it is warranted.

Sometimes you can turn your preconceived notions around. I had a client named James who was having trouble communicating his value to his colleagues. He was particularly peeved because a close coworker did less work but was able to trumpet his accomplishments more frequently in the presence of higher-ups—a classic Brag Better scenario. We discussed how he could showcase his value. James loved numbers instead of words, and would have much rather just buried his head in his spreadsheets. At my advice, instead of feeling jealous of his coworker who was more at ease bragging, James enlisted his colleague to help. He said, "I am really proud of this model I made last week. Are you open to sharing it in the meeting?"

At first, the colleague asked him why he couldn't do it himself. I told James he was just going to have to eat crow and tell his coworker why he was asking—that he admired how he shared his work. His coworker felt flattered and agreed to help James. That foray allowed James to dip a toe into being more vocal in meetings, and eventually showcase his work himself to the higher-ups. Months later, when he was comfortable enough, he did it on his own and with his own spin—using stats and numbers, the way he loved to communicate.

## BRAGGING BY SITUATION

Let me share more examples of bragging in some additional situations, such as in the break room, with a higher-up at a networking event, or with a peer at happy hour.

Take the time to craft a few brags in advance. List three or four situations where you'd like to be prepared with a brag. Now think about the following questions:

- What information would you like to get across?
- How much time do you have?
- What will be seen as the most valuable skill or asset to the person you're talking to?
- What is an accomplishment that you would like to highlight?

Now, take the answers into consideration as you prepare to write out a brag for each of your chosen situations. Once you've crafted each and made them sound like something you would naturally say, take the time to memorize them. You may not deliver them verbatim, but memorization will allow you to have a high comfort level with each of them.

## REITERATE, REFINE, AND EVOLVE

It will take time to make these techniques your own. Some of this might feel so incredibly awkward, which is fine when you're learning something new (you should see me with any new form of technology). It takes thought to decide how you want to share your accomplishments in a way that feels unique to you. Your method doesn't have to be the most unique in the world; it only has to be effective and further your goals. Whatever strategy you go with, it should be reflective of you. Focus on finding the perfect middle ground—phrases primed for bragging success combined with your own words that will express what you want to be known for.

Collect feedback wherever you can. Some feedback comes when you notice how you felt—good or bad—after you used a particular turn of phrase. Feedback can also come from others. If you notice a smile, nod, or eye-widening with a particular frame of brag, note that, too. If you know where and how to look, feedback makes itself available to you. I wish there were more shortcuts, but finding your voice in print, in particular, will take a lifetime. I know that mine has evolved and will continue to do so, and so will yours.

I got good at pitching my work and business from constantly refining my messaging for almost a decade, and I continue to refine it. If I introduced myself in a way that felt good at a particular conference, I'd take note of the words I used. If I added in a new sentence or changed the phrasing and felt it didn't land, I'd take note of that as well. I'm still refining it. I do this in speeches, too. Especially when a joke lands well or I use a new example and can see in real time how an audience is responding.

I can tell you about clients' journeys, but everyone's journey with his or her voice is personal. The way I talk about myself and my work shifts a lot and has transformed over the past decade. And it will keep transforming, considering that I am only thirty-three.

About ten years ago, I ran a humorous dating blog (the real fans might know) where my voice was much more outrageous, outlandish, and brash than I consider it to be now. I grew as I wrote, eventually to a point where the voice on that site was no longer mine. Eventually, I had to leave her be and forge a new path for a voice I wanted to communicate to the world. But sometimes I do miss her, and her bravery. I look back at some of the things I wrote and realize that as a fearless, kinda dumb twenty-three-year-old, I didn't have context for anything and just let things fly out of my mouth. It was fun then, but it doesn't work now, not with what I'm trying to accomplish.

My professional voice and the way I describe my business has also drastically evolved and morphed into what it is today. Nearly ten years ago I would've said something like, "I'm a digital strategist that also does PR." Now I say "I'm an entrepreneur who is passionate about visibility and voice, particularly for women. I speak and train around bragging, and my company trains leadership." Much different. That's because I practiced it for almost a decade, messed up a bunch, and saw some things work. It takes time, so give yourself time. For all I know, I could be a kooky dog writer in my later years and have a totally different voice (please let this happen as a retirement plan). As your brags evolve, so will you. We are all works in progress, all the time.

## *Ready, Set, Go!*

- **Now that you've decided you want more visibility, ask yourself the following questions (write down a two- or three-sentence answer for each):**
  - What do you want?
  - Why do you want it?
  - How do you think you'll get it?

- **Pick three people from different parts of your circle (a family member, a close friend, someone you're friendly with, a current coworker, a past coworker, or someone you know only from social media) and ask them the following:**
    - What do you think I do?
    - How would you explain my job?
    - What would you tell someone else about my career and work?
- **Practice bragging to your boss.**
- **Practice bragging to a coworker friend.**

# Part 2

# THE CAMPAIGN OF YOU

Long ago, when I was running FinePoint as a public relations company and I considered myself more of a traditional publicist, I realized that PR was a perfect weapon to get people to feel good about themselves when they discussed their accomplishments. I discovered that the activities of publicists—the things I was doing all day, every day, like packaging, pitching, forming stories, and garnering visibility—were all tremendously valuable when done for yourself. I started to wonder why nobody had leveraged these skills to help individuals, and *Brag Better* was born.

By borrowing from a publicist's playbook and skill set, you can create yourself as a shiny package, thus alleviating a lot of the strain and anxiety around Bragging Better. It allows you to step outside of yourself and consider the bigger story you're telling. It gives you confidence without it feeling so personal. It's like having an alter ego of sorts, a "projected self" that you have total control over and will launch in your Campaign of You.

A lot of people don't know what publicists do—or worse, they make fun of them. The mostly misogynist representation of PR people is as sleazy, dumb women. It's incredibly frustrating and false. Publicists think about how to package a story and how to tell it so that people pay attention. They simply craft a great narrative and hound you to pay attention. Why wouldn't someone admire that?

This is what you have to do for yourself: Figure out how you're going to package your story, your wins, and the best parts of you, and then how you're going to get people to pay attention. Acting as your own PR rep means that you must use a multifaceted approach that takes a range of contexts and audiences into consideration and tells the authentic stories that will entice them. You'll want to run a multi-armed Campaign of You.

Even if you don't plan to do your own public relations (hiring a good publicist is worth the money!), it is important to understand the tricks of the trade. If you learn to think like a publicist, you will upgrade your communication skills when delivering brags. I'm going to help you with your PR mindset so you know how to slip brags seamlessly into your PR process.

## UNAFRAID TO ASK FOR ATTENTION

The most important thing that you can borrow from a publicist's tool belt is being unafraid to ask for attention and recognition. That's part of what makes PR people so great—their directness and their ability to cut through the crap and get what they need for their client. Putting themselves out there all the time is a huge part of the gig—and the scariest part of Bragging Better. Half the battle here is getting over the fear of putting yourself out there, making asks, and pitching yourself. You will have to practice over and over again. Sometimes you will suck at it, as I have. But it's all part of the process.

Visibility can feel good, and then bad, then good again. Sometimes all in one day. It's important to know how to harness those feelings and also use them for success. Public relations skills are instances of Bragging Better. Each time that I have been able to get behind a story that I tell others about my work in a way that is planned, tight, and digestible, it has led to success.

Here's an example of it not working because I didn't have it right and tight. When I first started FinePoint, I was doing digital strategy work. In 2010, particularly in DC, "digital strategist" didn't mean much to those I wanted to hire me. Because of my own bias, I had stayed away from using the word "publicist" for many years. Except that's what I was. The second I started calling myself a "digital publicist," people began to hire me. I wasn't getting behind what I was actually doing and using industry terms for it. I was beating around the bush, trying to find my own vocabulary to describe essentially what was PR. I didn't need to reinvent the wheel.

In the next mini chapters, we're going to go through the pieces of the Campaign of You: introductions, pitching, public speaking, caring for your connections, and knowing when *not* to brag. Consider me your campaign co-manager.

# 6

# Résumés, Bios, Headshots, and Personal Websites

Your résumé, biography, and headshot are the low-hanging fruit that will help you begin your Bragging Better journey now. Your résumé is a baseline key spot to be proud, loud, and strategic. It exists to highlight everything awesome you've done. People expect to see it all—awards, recognition, past big projects. Throw it all in there and showcase your work. If you are just starting out, switching careers, or trying to level up—that's okay. Let your eagerness, motivation, and work ethic show on paper. Please, please put awards on there. Use your résumé as a trophy shelf.

Your résumé will continue to be a baseline indicator of work history and who you are in the professional world. I don't see it changing anytime soon. It's still necessary to upload or present your résumé for any job opportunity, even if you're a shoo-in. It's also the perfect place to Brag Better because everyone *expects* you to brag on a résumé. While other parts of the job application process are also important, like submitting writing samples and recommendations, your résumé shows who you are, where you've come from, and where you'd like to go. You are the one calling the shots.

Think about anything you might be leaving out. I was helping a friend with her résumé, and I noticed she didn't include an extremely prestigious award she had recently won. That award is a huge deal in her industry. It's the crown jewel of awards in what she does. She felt showy and uncomfortable including it. (Did I have a message for her!) I told her how much that particular award mattered, not only to her and for her work, but also among her contemporaries. It was an award that would immediately change the perception of someone in her line of work. It would elevate her status in their eyes more than almost anything else. She got the message.

## Spell Out Your Previous Work History

Today, titles don't mean squat. These days everyone seems to be a vice president. My dog is the VP of my house. Even if you have a title, you need to explain exactly what you do and exactly how you got there. If I'm reading your résumé, I want to know what you did, who you managed, and what kind of a big deal it is to get the title that you earned. Be very clear, concise, and detailed. Remember, all you're listing is facts.

- Instead of saying you "worked on a project," say:
  - "I led a team of ten on a project for the data management division of my company. We were tasked with creating a new strategy for our client, and as a result we delivered a comprehensive plan that our client loved and implemented. The new plan saved our client $20,000."

- Instead of saying you "were in a leadership" role, say:
  - "I managed a team of twenty people, and I reported directly to our CTO. I consistently received feedback on my helpful and direct management style, and I helped our CTO understand the needs of more junior employees."
- Instead of saying you "work on diversity efforts" at your company, say:
  - "I am responsible for making sure we highlight all kinds of voices at the company. I put together a panel of women of color to discuss what it was like working in advertising. It was enlightening for the entire staff and made everyone think deeply about the experiences of others in the workplace and move forward together as a brand."

This additional detail is crucial because many people work for themselves and thus make up their own titles. It can be very frustrating for those in more traditional hierarchical job systems, so be sure to show up for yourself and your title. Go overboard even if you think it is too much detail. It's not, I promise.

You have to make everyone's job as easy as possible. You need to set them up to easily and clearly brag about you. Fortunately, bragging is just stating facts. I am positive that you have those facts in spades.

## Bio Revamp

Your bio is a classic place to Brag Better, too. It's an asset, it's a no-brainer, and I'll explain why. A bio can help you get hired, gain visibility, and win you serious respect. If a journalist or recruiter cannot figure out who you are in under thirty seconds (because you have six different bios in six different places), you've lost your chance. Your bio is a crucial way to introduce yourself, especially online.

## THREE TYPES OF BIOS

Everyone needs a long, short, and two-line bio. They all need to match so that someone can immediately deduce who you are, and you can stay consistent and strong in your message.

- **Long bio:** About a page long (and includes everything). Your long bio helps determine what to boil down for a short bio, and then the short bio determines what to include in the two-line bio. Your long bio can be placed under your LinkedIn introduction, on a personal website under the "About You" tab, or somewhere else where space allows. Wherever you have the freedom and reign to put as much as possible, that's where it goes.
- **Short bio:** About a paragraph long (and includes only your best brags). Your short bio works for a presentation, at a conference, or on a work project.
- **Two-line bio:** The most succinct description of who you are, what you do, and what you stand for. It can be hard to write about yourself in only two lines, but by creating long and short bios, you'll understand the two to three pieces you cannot leave out for the shortest description. A two-line bio is a key summary of who you are. It gives someone the chance to be able to tell quickly and consistently what you do. Your two-line bio goes in all of your social media and after any article you write.

All your bios must match at all times. Don't forget this. They all need to complement one another to be a strong part of building that mosaic of who you are.

## DOS AND DON'TS

***Ditch hobbies or playful references, unless they reinforce your goals.***

If your dog is part of your brand (hello, Bean!), then you can incorporate it where appropriate. But understand that this is more of a traditional brag format. Save the "quirks" for a personal site.

I see women executives attempt to humanize themselves or seem less threatening by including references to gardening or other activities—stop that. This takes away from your more impressive accomplishments that should be there. Unless your startup has something to do with plants, remove it.

Think about what a white male executive would do in that situation. I think you know the answer.

***Include relevant hyperlinks.***

Don't assume that someone will read your bio, see something you've done, open a browser tab, Google that accomplishment, search through the results, and then read about it. That's too much work. You need to present it all and make it easy for them to click on it.

***Don't use weak verbs or passive voice.***

When someone uses the passive voice in a bio, it always feels to me like they're trying to downplay his or her achievements. The point of your bio is to emphasize your achievements. You are a person who has done things, so you need to write it that way—like you are proud and like you mean it. Another type of downplaying is using verbs that suggest you are "trying" or "attempting" to do something, be that change an industry or work with an idea. That makes it sound like you've already failed. You are not attempting to do it, you are doing it.

***Use your last name to describe yourself, not your first name or "I."***

"William is an expert in iambic pentameter and revenge plots" does not sound as professional as saying that "Shakespeare" is an expert in those things. Not only is using your last name more professional, it's also more memorable since last names tend to be more distinct than first names.

***Creative titles confuse people.***

What about referring to yourself as a "ninja" or "rock star"? Drop it. While that might work in technology or the startup world, it won't read as professionally in more traditional industries. You want your bio to be something that travels across industries and across all audiences.

***Include calls to action.***

Your bio is a marketing tool for your business and for your career. If you speak, link to how to book you for a speaking gig. If you consult, provide links to an initial consult call. If you offer an online course, link to the course. It would be a waste to have someone read your bio and not become a potential customer. Your bio is the ultimate place to Brag Better. People expect brags from it, so give it to them.

## Headshots

You need a new headshot every time you cut your hair or change your appearance noticeably in some way—if you get glasses or have Lasik, change your hair color, or anything else significant. I suggest headshots every two years. Not everyone likes to get their picture taken, so I suggest paying for professional hair and makeup. Your hair should be done however you normally wear it.

Here are my headshot recommendations:

- **Outfits:** Wear solid colors with minimal jewelry, maybe one dressed-up outfit and one more casual.
- **Hair and makeup:** Spend on hair and makeup if it makes you feel good.
- **Shot list:** Most professional photographers will take a number of photos in various positions and locations. Here are some standard shots:
  - Head-on, smiling
  - Head-on, not smiling
  - Turned to the side, arms crossed, looking at camera, smiling
  - Turned to the side, arms crossed, looking at camera, not smiling
  - Action/orating photo
  - Inside head-on shot
  - Outside head-on shot
  - Action/walking shot

## Your Personal Website

Many clients think that a personal website is comprised of images of them dancing across the screen, with a banner of their face and music playing. It is not (unless this fits with your brand, in which case, go for it—like if you're a millennial and you remember the site Hamster Dance, which is self-explanatory).

A personal website is crucial. You need your own territory on the internet with your own design, accomplishments, and personality. I have seen the lack of a personal website hold back many clients, particularly those who want to speak more. Describe the audiences and organizations you've spoken for, and share a highlight reel of your best talks. If you have personal hobbies and other things you care about, this is a good place to share those.

Your personal website is a visual representation of you, and that is a strong pitch because humans are visual creatures. You can write about your experience endlessly, but showing the world is even more effective. In interviews with six different hiring managers, journalist Aja Frost found that all six agreed that personal websites were extremely helpful.

I had a client named Jamie. She had done a ton of speaking, but didn't put it on her personal site so that event organizers, bookers, or conference attendees could see. She wanted to do more speaking, but she couldn't easily point to her experience. So much of Bragging Better is handing a package of you on a silver platter to those in power, making someone's route to saying yes to you that much easier. Unsurprisingly, she didn't get a speaking gig she wanted because even though she had the chops, she didn't have the showmanship. The organizers couldn't tell that this wasn't her first rodeo; they thought she was too inexperienced. They went with someone who was actually less experienced than Jamie, simply because that person did a better job of showcasing the little experience they had.

Your personal website is the only place online where you have total control. On social media you're beholden to your audience's chosen boxes and visuals. On your company's website, you are housed within a larger organization. Your personal website is a living résumé. It shows rather than tells. Your website is the one-stop shop of you. It is a crucial stop for someone trying to hire you, write about you, or invest in you. Plus, it can be fun (but again, this is what I do for a living, so my idea of fun might be a little different from yours).

My personal website displays a combination of the things I care about—color and humor, my dog, writing, women and voice, and consignment and resale fashion. It looks like me, too. I worked carefully on a design that was playful while still authoritative, beautiful while practical. Every part of it is intentional.

Think about your professional goals, and then about what you can put on your page to highlight why and how you can get there. Personal websites get people jobs. I once hired someone for a project because of her website, and I'm positive I'm not the only one. There are so many things you can't communicate online, but if you're able to give someone a sense of that X factor, or the magic of your personality, you are in a position of power.

You have no excuse and I'm not letting you off the hook. There are a ton of easy-to-use platforms for creating a personal site. A lot of these services are free (at least at the basic level) and make producing your website a lot easier than it looks. This is the biggest reason clients tell me that they don't have their own websites—fear of the technical aspects. You are missing out on money and power without one, so let me light a fire under your butt to do it or at least begin the process.

About fifteen years ago, I interviewed for an internship at a PR firm. I don't remember the name of the firm, the name of the founder, or what we talked about (save for that their kitchen area had diner booths?). The thing I remember, clear as day, was that the CEO said to me, "If you don't remember anything else, at least buy the domain of your name." After that meeting, I did. And now I will say the same to you, with similar fervor: buy every iteration of your domain name—.com, .org, .net, .me. You never know what will happen; someone with a name similar to yours could become famous (for good or bad reasons), or someone could potentially harm your online reputation by using your name in a URL.

If you have a common name, also purchase domains with your middle initial in case you decide to use your middle initial professionally. By owning the domains sooner rather than later, you avoid another worst-case scenario—someone squatting on your domain name and trying to sell it back to you. YouTube queen Jenna Marbles talked on her podcast about not owning her own domain name. Someone snapped it up and tried to sell it back to her for six figures. She refused and still uses jennamarblesblog.com. Note that jennamarbles.com was purchased by someone two days after her first viral video. I never want anyone to be in this position.

For your personal site, use the simplest URL possible. A cheeky phrase with an unusual URL might seem cool to you, but you also want your work to be accessible across industries. It will confuse people to have to search for something that seems unrelated to your name. Think about the least tech-savvy person accessing your website (sometimes that person is me!). You don't want them to be driven away by too many unusual bells and whistles.

You might prefer that only the cool kids look at your website, but you want to cast as wide a net as possible to promote yourself and never leave anyone out. Some of the most powerful, wealthy individuals and industries need a simple setup or design. I've made the mistake of wanting only the cool kids to check out my "super cool" website. Guess who often has the deep pockets? It's not just the "cool kids."

# 7

# Introductions

I recall with absolute horror a particular time that I blundered an introduction. Like, I *really* ate it. I was at South by Southwest in Austin, Texas, at the technology portion of the conference. I remember meeting the friend of a well-known woman (okay, she was cool and famous) that I had admired for a long time. This semifamous woman invited me to a party at the conference, where I smashed my finger in the door on the way in, and still to this day often can't feel the top of my ring finger. I was really killing it that night. I felt cool by association though, at least for a few minutes. This woman introduced me to her famous friend, let's call her Lexi, who had a technology company that was doing very well, and I hoped she could be a potential client.

It was my first time at a major conference as an entrepreneur, and I was trying to "play it cool." Never take this advice. Being cool is way overrated and either comes naturally or doesn't. I will always be a dork; it just is what it is.

Everyone was there to network, and I kept walking the line between a serious businessperson and whatever version of nonchalant I thought I should be.

It didn't help my cause that I had taken some bad business development advice from an expert whose industry differed greatly from mine. This expert was in a much slower and more serious (finance and estate planning) business than mine, which required much more of a long-game approach to getting clients. A line he often used was to tell someone he had just met that he wanted "to shoot the breeze and talk business later." I laugh thinking about this now, because it's also wildly male. And so wildly not me. Also "shooting the breeze" should be reserved for seventy-year-old white men on a golf course.

At the party, Lexi began to describe and pitch her business to me and ask about mine. I cut her off, tossed my hair, and said a version of "Let's just have fun and talk about business later." I thought I was crushing it and that she would think I was oh so cool. I'll never forget the look she gave me, which was a mixture of confusion and disdain. The conversation was over. She walked away, and we never spoke again. I knew immediately I had taken the wrong approach, completely torched my chances of doing work together, and also just revealed to her what a true dork I was.

I blundered because I wasn't firm on my own style of introduction, I didn't consciously pick my words, and I certainly didn't read the room. I missed a key opportunity.

## First Impressions Matter

First impressions really do matter. I chose to give one that was not true to who I was, nor was it thoughtful or effective. Researchers have spent years studying the many ways that we make split-second judgments about other people. Sometimes the results of this research are obvious: A 2011 study found that people who wear name-brand clothing are perceived as wealthier (though the labels had no effect on their perceived attractiveness, friendliness, or trustworthiness). Often the research shows just how much we stereotype others, as in a 2008 study showing that people with glasses are perceived as being more intelligent. Even with those findings, though, it's important to remember that first impressions aren't about presenting a shiny, false persona. Authenticity matters, too. A series of studies in 2005 found that when people needlessly use long, fancy words in an attempt to sound intelligent, it actually backfires, and they are perceived as being *less* intelligent.

When you are introducing yourself, you are making a first impression, so it's an opportunity to brag in a controlled way. Each introduction you make gives you an opportunity to not only win someone over, but also get a new piece of business, refine your message, and help someone else Brag Better, too. I'd say it's one of the *most* important takeaways from *Brag Better*, at least when it comes to tactics.

It doesn't matter if you're an intern or chairman of the board, your introduction counts. Being prepared is what's going to make your brag or introduction land best. Judith Humphrey, a communications expert writing in *Fast Company*, lets us in on a little secret, "Those who are excellent at off-the-cuff speaking have a secret: They don't wing it; they prepare. As paradoxical as it may sound, preparing to be spontaneous is key. In fact, the word 'impromptu' derives from the Latin *in promptu*, meaning 'in readiness.'"

Practicing your introduction can help you elevate it in order to take the next step. You can take "Nice to meet you, I work in marketing" to "So great to connect, I work in marketing and run a team of ten. I'd love to talk to you more about management and show you a bit about how I make sure my team's projects are some of the most successful in our division." Be prepared because you never know who is on the other side of your handshake.

I'll say it again: *You never know who is on the other side of your handshake.*

I certainly learned from my mistakes, but I also learned from the chances I continue to take with having a tight, solid introduction that I've practiced. I was at an event for an industry I care a lot about—sustainable fashion. One of the panelists was an icon in the fashion industry and someone whose extensive career I had admired for a long time. After the panel ended, I went up to her to fangirl, basically. I told her how much I admired her and that I was so excited to just be in her presence. Instead of blowing me off, she asked me what I did. I told her that I represented women in positions of power (succinct; considering the audience, I knew it would be of interest to her as a woman in a position of power). She said, "Well, maybe I should hire you." I screamed a little (I think it came out as kind of a squeal). And the great thing? She did! (*High-five self.*)

## Choose Your Words Wisely

Choose your words wisely, as in, give them some thought and practice in front of a mirror. A lot of people think this might be "conniving" or "calculated." I'm like, hello, yeah, I'm calculating an opportunity for myself. Why wouldn't I try to be prepared?

I will use myself as an example. Each of my introductions in the following scenarios is for a specific audience.

The three introductions are similar, but vary greatly among audience, tone, and mood.

### INTRODUCTION 1

***Audience:*** Executives

*My name is Meredith Fineman and I run a company called FinePoint, a leadership and professional development company that trains CEOs and founders, irrespective of industry, on visibility and voice. Leadership as celebrity is more important and lucrative than ever, and brands' CEOs are public figures. Therefore, crafting the right public persona is key to making sure you're not missing any opportunities or leaving money on the table.*

Here's why it works: I know that executives want to hear what's in it for them—money. What can I do for them specifically? What are the consequences of not hiring me?

### INTRODUCTION 2

***Audience:*** Young Women's Conference

*My name is Meredith Fineman and I run a company called FinePoint, which helps people find their voices, particularly women. I care that women, no matter their age, point in career, or outlook, feel good talking about their professional accomplishments and bragging. That's why I'm here to speak to you.*

Here's why it works: I want to motivate an audience, speak to non-executives, and instill a sense of confidence in the listeners. I want this particular age group—let's say emerging college students—to feel empowered moving into the world. I also want my audience to know why they should care about listening to me.

**INTRODUCTION 3**

***Audience:*** Potential Client

*My name is Meredith Fineman and I run a company called FinePoint, a leadership and professional development company that trains leaders across industries how to present their best selves and succeed in business. Each client, and at this point I've trained hundreds, comes to me with a specific set of visibility issues that we work through based on tried-and-true strategies and exercises that I've developed over the past near decade.*

Here's why it works: I am proving why a client would need to hire me and emphasizing what I've done for other people. I'm making the case for spending money on me—especially given how long I've been doing this and with how many other people.

TRY THIS OUT with your introduction: Pick a few different audiences and practice tailoring to them. As a starting point, think back to your notes about being strategic. When you listed your goals and audiences, those are now a resource for this exercise. This will help refine your message and make you more effective. I have been practicing these introductions for almost a decade, and I still iterate on them. It's a process. Don't be afraid to do it in the mirror, either. You have a great audience.

## The Mechanics of an Introduction

There are some crucial elements that make a good first impression, beginning with your eyeballs. They matter a lot—and science reinforces this. A 2006 study from the *Applied Ergonomics* journal found that eye contact between a sales presenter and his audience significantly enhanced the audience's ability to remember details from the sales presentation later. The better eye contact you maintain, the more you are going to be remembered and believed.

Look. People. In. The. Eye. A roundup of eye contact research by the British Psychological Society found that "we tend to form rather low opinions of people who persistently avoid our gaze, assuming that they are less sincere and, at least if they're female, less conscientious. Conversely, we're more likely to believe statements made by a person who looks us in the eye." Show them your peepers, please.

Then there's the classic signaler of showing up for yourself: your handshake. I do not allow any limp noodles. Nothing is grosser than someone's slightly sweaty, lifeless hand meeting yours in a professional context. It immediately tells the other person not to take you seriously. Research backs this up, especially when it comes to women. A 2008 study in the *Journal of Applied Psychology* found that "the relationship between a firm handshake and interview ratings may be stronger for women than for men." Research from the University of Alabama found that "a firm handshake may be an effective form of self-promotion for women." Another study looked at pairs of business school students performing simulated negotiations and found that the pairs who had been told to shake hands at the beginning of their negotiations ended with better mutual outcomes. In other words, people like handshakes! They help facilitate openness and collaboration. You don't have to crush someone's paw, but you do have to make your hand act like it wants to be there.

Then there are elements that are mandatory and memorable. Having an interesting business card makes you more memorable. Business cards are a formality, and one I don't think will go away as quickly as everyone thinks. The same goes for a written professional thank-you note—classy touches that leave an impression.

## DON'T WING IT

You're self-sabotaging if you decide to wing an introduction. You're also missing an opportunity to connect more deeply by not taking it seriously. Any time I decide to wing something, it doesn't go well.

| Instead of Winging It with . . . | Try This |
|---|---|
| A client on a call | Take fifteen minutes to research a little bit more about them beyond the scope of your work directly. Opening with a hello and an introduction to your work, plus a bit about them that isn't common knowledge, goes a long way. It makes it clear that you've done the research and are here to be a great asset. |
| A new vendor | If you're meeting in person, tout your expertise but also make it clear you will serve as a bridge between your companies. Offer yourself up as a resource and leave time for questions. |
| A new colleague | Take a minute to learn about him or her and offer your guidance and expertise. |

I've gotten good at pitching—and your introduction is a micro-pitch—because I do it all day, every day and have for nearly a decade. I play and iterate, but I also show up for every person I meet. Take a minute and think about the person you're meeting, and how you can relay or relate your experience to them. This kind of awareness begets opportunities, endears you to others, and passes on the kind of spirit you should want to carry throughout your career.

I once met someone very powerful and had read up on one of his more obscure hobbies, which happened to be something I was interested in. I mentioned that to him instead of saying all the same things he likely gets day in and day out. Not only did it snag his attention, but I was also able to connect in a way that I wouldn't have if I had just stuck with classic shoptalk. Then we didn't have to drone on about work; we got to talk about a hobby we both love.

We all get tired sometimes and fall back into checking off the boxes when meeting someone new. But that energy you bring is infectious. "I work in marketing for [X] company" can easily become "I run marketing at [X] company, and I manage a team of seven. I'm currently working on a project for our new product, [X]. It's really exciting! Here's my card." Big difference.

# 8

# Pitching

A genius, hilarious, successful friend of mine reached out to tell me some great news. She had pitched a major outlet on a thorough freelance essay using her expertise in international relations. This household-name publication was going to run the article in the coming weeks and compensate her well. I was thrilled—it was a news organization that takes very little outside writing. I was impressed but not surprised. She is one of the smartest and most thoughtful people I know. I couldn't wait to see her name in print.

I ran into her a few weeks later at a party. I wanted to toast her and asked her when the article was going to appear. She told me that she was crushed. At the last second, the outlet decided not to publish her article and showcase her hard work. I knew I could fix it, though, and I snapped into publicist mode. I asked her to share her "pitch list" with me so I could help make any connections possible. I expected to hear that she had pitched to a dozen or so alternative outlets. My mouth dropped when she told me there was no list, that she had only contacted that outlet. But she was sure nobody would take it now, and she was gutted, despondent, and being very dramatic about it.

I wanted to shake her. Pitching and constant rejection is a publicist's day-to-day work. I've written for a lot of media entities, but the majority of my writing, and the work of my clients, has been rejected first. It's how you learn, it's how you get better, and it's how you frame sharing your accomplishments. Become your own best PR person and keep on pitching. Do you know how many times I had to pitch *Brag Better*? A lot!

My friend, who was not in the public relations industry, saw this rejection as the be-all and end-all. She was brilliant and successful, and yet she saw it as the end of the road. I saw it as a starting point. She sent me her piece, and we went over about ten other outlets she could reach out to. I helped her craft pitches that framed her article and her work in a great light, and she got a few bites. Eventually, the article ran—in a totally different outlet, with some framing and finessing that fit that magazine's style. It was not a failure; it was a chance to Brag Better and learn the hard way that pitching is a skill you can acquire to propel yourself and your work.

Natalia Oberti Noguera is founder and CEO of Pipeline Angels, a network of women investors that's changing the face of angel investing and creating capital for women and nonbinary femme social entrepreneurs. She emphasizes that pitching is not as black-and-white as a lot of us think. She remarked: "I remember when Dahna Goldstein, founder of PhilanTech [a Pipeline Angels portfolio company that was acquired by Altum], shared with me how 'Pitching is the start of a conversation.' I love this perspective. Pitching isn't always a zero-sum game of either you win or you lose. Even if an entrepreneur doesn't secure funding after pitching, the people in the room may be able to provide helpful feedback and/or introductions, including to potential investors and customers/users. Practice makes pitching—and bragging—better." Oberti Noguera hears pitches all day, nearly every day and she asserts that it's something you should iterate on constantly. I know that I do.

Pitching is selling yourself and asking for something in return. It can mean pitching your business to a prospective client, pitching your article to a journalist for a guest post, or simply pitching an idea to your boss to gauge their interest. Technically, it means "a form of words used when trying to persuade someone to buy or accept something." Pitching is an art form perfected by publicists, and it is key to Bragging Better.

## Your Story

The most important part of pitching yourself and your work is the story you tell and the timeliness of it. Humans digest storytelling—that's how we process information, learn to form opinions, and see the world. The better a story holds our attention, the more likely we are to recall it, tell it to others, and remember it for years to come. Every great PR pro knows this—and here's what they do to tell the best story possible.

## BE SPECIFIC

You need to be as concrete and specific as possible. You may know that Bragging Better can be hard, but if I don't include something like the following in my description, it's just not as effective: "Have you ever been in a business development meeting and not been able to sell yourself or felt bad about your pitch? Well, that's what I'm here to fix." Not only does a turn of phrase like this put my work into terms people can understand, but it also allows them to empathize with the problem and consider it for themselves. Or if I say, "Do you ever feel like there's someone in your industry that always gets the recognition, when you know more than they do? Aren't you sick of that?" (This always works resoundingly.) Sometimes I lead with frustration around our environment, like, "Do you feel like everyone is yelling and we are rewarding them? I can help you navigate that system." (The answer is always yes.)

Pitching well demands that you use as many illustrative examples as you can so that people can latch on to you and your work. Make your stories specific, colorful, and thoughtful. Show, don't tell, or at least show *and* tell. We consume stories through vivid storytelling; you know that a key issue will be better remembered through a riveting Netflix documentary than through a series of wonky articles. It's how we process and remember things.

In a now-classic psychological experiment from the late 1960s, researcher Allan Paivio found that when people were shown a rapid series of images and words, they were better able to remember the images than the words. These findings and many similar studies led to what is known as the dual coding theory, which states that verbal and visual information are processed differently in our brains. The theory states that coding some piece of information both ways—using words and images—increases the odds that we will remember that information later. And even within the verbal realm, several studies have shown that concrete words are more memorable than abstract words. So when you're bragging about your accomplishments, make sure your story comes alive with vivid vocabulary and visual imagery.

## Successful Pitch Examples

Keep a pitch about yourself and your work short, sweet, and to the point. If it's in an email, write a short paragraph. You're hoping to get what you want with this paragraph, so that means handing your reader, editor, or recruiter your idea on a silver platter. Convey short, actionable information. Include key links so that the person reading your pitch is required to do no additional research. You want that other person to do as little as possible. Everyone's inboxes are overflowing, so the key, no matter who you're pitching, is to get your recipient the where, when, why, and how of the story of you as quickly as possible, with as little work as possible.

## Who's On the Other End?

Part of what makes a good PR person is understanding their audience, what they want to hear, and what their deep jungle nightmare of an inbox looks like. It helps to understand who you're talking to when you form connections, pitch your work, and Brag Better.

Have you ever thought about a journalist, conference booker, recruiter, or an important person's inbox? Yeah, it's a nightmare. It's likely full of random bad pitch emails, coupons, and junk. You need to stand out, but you also need to show that at the very least you care who you're emailing.

I blundered that really badly once. I still cringe thinking about it. At my first (and only) job working for someone else, I pitched seventy important, influential, terrifying mom bloggers and didn't *specify their names*. What I mean is, I began each pitch with "Dear [Blogger]" in *seventy* emails. It was the first major thing I had to do, and I royally messed up. If even one of those bloggers, with millions of readers, had decided to complain about the brand's research person, aka me, we would have been toast. I was horrified and ashamed. I sat for hours the day before Christmas break individually emailing each blogger, apologizing profusely, and praying that none would say anything about it online. I've now gotten those emails, and they're an immediate send to the trash. Care about someone's name, and care that you spell it correctly. All those sorts of mistakes remove you from the room where it happens before you can even turn the doorknob.

Pitching is specific to your network. Most publicists aren't talking to people they don't know. They use their network and ask for five minutes to talk about their client and what they can offer. As for the pitch itself, it should be brief, often just one sentence. If I were trying to pitch for a client or for myself, and the person I wanted to speak with was high up in the company or publication, I would try to find a mutual acquaintance who might be able to introduce us. For example, if I were trying to pitch *The Ellen DeGeneres Show*, I would check LinkedIn and email a group of my connections in California. I would ask if they knew anyone who works with the show and if they were open to passing along contact information or looping me in on an introduction email. Be sure to ask, "Are you open to introducing us?"

This moves the conversation forward, but leaves them the option to say no.

If your contact simply passes along the person's email address, ask if you can use the contact's name as a reference. If they say yes, then put their name in the subject line. That way, the email will have a higher likelihood of being opened.

If I'm pitching someone whose name I've been given by a contact, I might write:

> Subject: Via Meredith Fineman
>
> Meredith Fineman, who is a client, used to write for *Entrepreneur*. She reached out to her former editor and they sent along your information. Are you open to receiving pitches?

The most ideal situation is a "warm" introduction (about one degree or so of separation), so try to get as close to your final target as possible through your network. You want to be careful, though. In this day and age, people are connected via social media to others whom they don't know that well. Be sure to ask how close the connection is before you take the referral.

If you feel like you don't know anyone who can connect you to people or companies that you'd like to pitch, here are a couple of examples that I have used.

***For a client pitch:***

> Hi [NAME],
> I hope this finds you well. I loved your most recent piece on [insert something here]. I wanted to reach out to you about my client Dan and his new VR

technology startup. I know you often write about the intersection of virtual reality and our current lifestyles. Dan could be a great expert source or an interview. Are you open to chatting more?

*For my writing pitch:*

Hi [Editor],
I'm a big fan of [website], and I love how you blend humor and practical advice for young women. I'm a freelance writer of fifteen years [link to my work], and I have written pieces in the past that speak to your audience and your tone. Below are four story ideas. Let me know if you're open to these pitches and are interested in speaking about any of them further.

## The Most Important Part of a Pitch: The Why

Why should this person care? What's it to them? That might seem harsh, but that's crucial. I often sit on the other side of pitch emails, and I see companies mess up with long, copy-laden pitches that are clearly pasted from a large marketing document. I am bored. It has nothing to do with me; who I am hasn't been considered, and I am not being offered anything interesting. You just put me on a long list of writers that cover business and women's issues, sometimes travel. This not only doesn't work, but also ends up having the opposite effect—it creates negative sentiment.

You need to make your pitch worth someone else's time. Your pitch should be designed to advance your career, but you need to make it worthwhile to them. Maybe they desperately need your skill set and expertise. Maybe they need your voice on their panel. Think about that. You need to assume that someone who is receiving these pitches is receiving them by the thousands. Yours need to stand out, and they need to be solid and thoughtful.

You also need a call to action. If I get a pitch that's eight paragraphs about a new hotel opening, I'm like, "Cool, but what do you want me to do with that?" I'm not going to call my friend and say, "Guess what? This new hotel is opening. Okay, bye!" Whether it's asking to get on a call, look over a document, or meet for coffee, busy people want to know what you want and fast.

## The Brag Breakdown with Fran Hauser: Deliver Your Unique Value

*Fran Hauser is a well-known investor and author who is regularly pitched for funding. She has learned a lot along the way about what makes a good pitch, but also what makes her own voice authentic.* The Myth of the Nice Girl *author breaks down how to find your own unique value.*

### You Are Just as Valuable as Someone "Big"

"Often, younger people tend to question what value they can offer somebody who's more senior than them. In reality, we almost always have something to offer; for young professionals in particular, you may have access to a network or community, knowledge of a social media platform, or functional expertise that could be very helpful to a person who is more 'senior' than you. There's always an opportunity to add value."

### Don't Just Ask, Offer

"A young woman recently reached out to me on LinkedIn. She had taken the time to research my portfolio and pointed out that there were several companies I funded that could use some social media help. She offered some ideas and also asked if I'd be willing to share advice with her. It really caught my attention. I'm much more likely to respond to this type of note, where someone offers a helpful opinion or idea, compared to a cold ask for a meeting or phone call."

## What Makes a Good Pitch

There are several crucial factors that make a pitch good. The pitch should be each of the following:

- **Concise:** Nothing is worse than a pitch that is too long. The ideal is about five sentences, *maybe* two paragraphs if you really need to. Get to the when, where, what, why, and "so what" as quickly as possible. Assume someone is reading this on his phone, on a packed subway car, late for work. With that mindset, what are you going to tell them as fast as possible? Only exactly what he needs to know. You can never be too concise.
- **Relevant:** If that person, who is sweating profusely on the subway car, cramped and anxious, is reading something irrelevant, then he is going to plunk your pitch directly into his trash folder, *and* it might make him mad. Your pitch needs to be relevant to the person reading it. Either it's a topic they cover or something they've written or spoken about, or they are the right point of contact within an organization. I've sat on the other end of that email, one that has nothing to do with me. Whether it's a subject I don't

write about, it isn't anything new or newsworthy, or I can tell I am just on a long list of people to pitch and it isn't tailored at all, receiving an email like that really pisses me off because it feels like a waste of my time. And I don't forget it.

- **Thoughtful:** A little bit of kindness and consideration goes a long, long way. It's important to not provide a laundry list and to be tight with your pitch. But it's also important to show someone you're pitching that you've read his or her work. It endears you to them and shows that you know who they are. Investor and author Fran Hauser sees a lot of founders miss out on including the key part of the pitch: themselves. Hauser says that when founders "start their pitch by talking about the product, they don't realize how important it is to talk about themselves. That emotional connection is so important." You don't want to be robotic. You want to connect with whomever you're pitching to.

  Back to the harried subway guy: He writes about technology. In the pitch he just received, someone told him they liked an article he wrote a few months back and showed they had read it. He just smiled and forgot it was a billion degrees in the crowded subway car.

- **Actionable:** What is the one thing you need? Can you describe it in one sentence? The worst thing is to receive a pitch with no action item. Whether you're asking for an article that you wrote to be published, or you're asking for an interview, or a spotlight in a company newsletter, you need to be clear about what you want. This is where directness comes in.

> Crazed subway guy needs to know what you need right now, because he's running to the office with coffee on his pants.

Treat everyone you're pitching like they're in a hurry on a cramped subway car in the middle of the summer. It will keep you on your toes, consistent, concise, thoughtful, and ready for anything.

## The Brag Breakdown with Luvvie Ajayi: How to Pitch Someone Important

*Cultural critic, best-selling author, digital strategist, and renowned speaker Luvvie Ajayi knows what cuts through the noise. As a popular fixture among many communities and online, Ajayi is constantly getting pitched by people wanting to get her attention—and only a few voices get it. Here is how to make a big ask.*

### The Formula Is Simple

"What breaks through the noise is people who are clear, confident, and concise."

### Keep It Brief

"Don't send anybody this giant tome. We don't necessarily need your whole life story to be able to know what you'd like and how we can help."

### Three Key Paragraphs

"I always tell people to send three paragraphs. Nothing more.

"The first paragraph is introducing yourself. Give me a short feel of your story. We need to know who these words are from. Let's say I'm sending an email pitch: 'Hi, my name is Luvvie Ajayi, I'm a writer, digital strategist, and speaker. I've been doing this work for about fifteen years, and I'm really passionate about making people think critically about the world and laugh while they're doing it.'

"The second paragraph needs to be how [you're] connected to the work. [Show them] you're familiar with their work and that you are sending this message [specifically to them] and not just cold emailing every random person that you see: 'I've been following your work for a few years.'

"The last paragraph is the ask. Be straightforward. Let's say my ask is 'I'd love to have a one-hour phone call with you.' The way the last paragraph should be phrased should be something like: 'I've definitely learned a lot from you. I would love to get a one-hour conversation with you on the phone where I ask you five questions that I have not been able to find in your work that you've put out so far.'"

### Where Can You Offer Value?

"Think about the value that you bring to the table. If you have difficulty emailing somebody you've never met, maybe the first thing you shouldn't do is ask for a favor. Be yourself. Offer yourself up and something you do that could be helpful to them. People are usually after me for things—[but] this person who's offering me something? That will let your email cut through the noise."

### Be Appreciative, Not Entitled

"[Close with] something that shows [you do] not feel entitled to the time but would appreciate it: 'Thank you for your consideration if things don't work out.' Even if I don't have the time, I will at least do something."

**Leave Out the Hand-Wringing**

"All the hand-wringing happens a lot when I get emails from women, especially young women. I want women to see what it's like for another woman to not constantly doubt herself and her words. I want more of us to be, like, 'Yes, I can ask this question, and if I get a no, a no will not kill me.'"

## SEE WHAT STICKS

You have to test the waters of your own narrative and see what sticks; that's the only way to improve and succeed. Many clients ask me my expectations, or what a journalist thinks if she hears pitch *x* versus *y*. I can only control so many factors and lean on my years of understanding stories and media, so I can't tell you which way the wind blows on a certain day in a certain email inbox. Some of this is also absolute chance and completely arbitrary. Why a story gets killed, or they don't use your quote, usually it has nothing to do with you and is more likely to do with the budget or space constraints or breaking news or something else entirely out of your control. The most important thing is to just begin.

## KEEP GOING

You can spend only so long on your end figuring out what the best story to tell about yourself and your work might be. I've told many different stories about myself and my business over the past decade, and I've learned when to tell each story, but that is only because I've made mistakes and told some bad stories. Perhaps I wasn't reading the room or had not figured out my audience. Start testing those waters, and as you modify your pitch you will learn a lot about what sticks. Sometimes what sticks goes beyond just numbers or a pretty picture.

### REJECTION IS KEY

That volume of pitching and getting used to rejection is crucial for learning to Brag Better. You would never get better if everyone always said yes. Being resilient through the nos and coming to terms with rejection make you a much stronger storyteller and professional. Each rejection will get easier over time. The more you throw out there, and the more you pick yourself back up and continue to tell your story, the more recognition you'll get. Now, you can't zoom into a decade of experience handling rejection overnight, but I think we should all try getting rejected a little more. It's an uncomfortable, awful, character-building experience.

Rejection is universal. Please remember this. You are in good company with J. K. Rowling, Oprah Winfrey, Meryl Streep, Sallie Krawcheck, Stephen King, Jay-Z, and anyone who has ever lived.

## Cultivate (and Care for) Your Connections

Public relations is also about relationships, almost exclusively. That's the main underlying thread that links all good PR people. Your day-to-day looks like cultivating contacts, making sure to connect with people, and then gracefully pitching them and asking for recognition. Sometimes relentlessly and ever-so-gently getting in their faces. I toe that line constantly. Because it's their moneymaker, publicists fiercely guard their press relationships and know how and when to ask and when to pull back.

This is tremendously helpful to use for your Campaign of You. Relationships are like a plant you can't let die (okay, so a succulent, because hopefully most of them are hard to kill). You need to water them every so often, maybe sing to them, and ask them how they're doing. This is part of what Bragging Better for yourself is—cultivating and maintaining key relationships, knowing when to brag, and knowing when to wait.

Start to think about who you're already connected to and where you might begin. Whenever you meet someone, email with someone, or see someone you admire, write down their name and contact information and save it. Every so often, I carefully go through the box of business cards of people I've met that I keep next to my desk. There are probably thousands of business cards at this point, and sometimes I keep them as a reminder of just how many people I've talked to regarding Brag Better and my work. It also reminds me, as it should remind you, to follow up, to ask people how they are doing, and to think about how you can serve them, too. This goes beyond what someone can do for you professionally—you never know where a networking relationship or professional introduction might take you. My networking relationships have led me to deep friendships, partnerships on projects, and even mentorships.

Making connections and asking someone to speak with you takes guts but has a lot of rewards. Many years ago, I reached out to a collaborator named Jess. I was a little bit jealous of her—she seemed to be doing really cool projects in DC, and I wanted to work at that level, too. I cold messaged her on Facebook, complimenting her on her work, and asked if I could have coffee with her. Our meeting blossomed into a decade-long friendship. Jess is also the best publicist I know. She did not need to pitch me to say that. I gained a best friend, all because I was willing to reach out to her.

Not everyone is a people person. I've staked a career on being one, but all you need is one friend, one serious contact, or one networking session to begin. I'm not telling you to become a publicist, unless that's what you want to do. I'm only asking you to think like one.

Relationships are a two-way street, too. Don't think you're the one doing all the taking; it's far from that. You'll need to consider what you can do for them, too. Giving your time, advice, or thoughts to someone you meet is highly gratifying. I am always sure to ask people what they might need, even if I'm not asking for something. Helping people feels good and puts some really great karma into the world. Plus, everyone can learn something from someone else. Just because you're trying to get to someone senior doesn't mean they cannot learn from you. Your accomplishments are worth talking about, but also valuable no matter what stage you're coming from.

# 9

# Salary Negotiations

Salary negotiations are very tough and scary. It's uncomfortable, for both you and often the people sitting across the table from you. You have to enter these situations prepared, know what you want, know how you're going to justify it, and also do all of this within a single meeting and likely a bureaucracy. The stakes are high for this brag.

I counseled a now well-known woman on her salary many years ago, when she was much more junior. When we talked for the first time, it was immediately apparent to me that she was going to be a shining star. She had it all—experience, a sharp mind, a quick wit, and the look—and yet she was heinously underpaid. She worked for a small media startup and the working environment was pretty brutal. Long hours, few benefits, mistreatment from management, and the low pay all combined to make her miserable, but she wanted to keep this job because she felt like it was a big break for her. She was going in for a yearly review and a salary negotiation, and she wanted a salary that was in the low six figures. She knew the number she wanted, but she was afraid to ask for it and didn't know how to make the request. She was terrified of moving from five to six figures, but she knew it was what she wanted and deserved given how quickly her work was becoming known in her industry.

To prepare her for the negotiation, I had her write out her value, literally. She wrote out what had improved since she began working for the company and shared metrics to back it up; she described the unique assets she brought to the table that other employees did not have; she shared industry comps showing what other people in her position made. These were essentially her brags laid out on paper, with comparable information, so that her employer understood just what kind of value she delivered through her accomplishments.

I had her compile all of that information into a two-page handout. Since a salary negotiation is very similar to a pitch, I wanted her to have "marketing" materials that backed up her assertions about her value to the company. Whether it's a PowerPoint presentation or a two-page report, she needed to show her value in concrete numbers, with a physical reminder of what she's done for the company. We put together a mini presentation, which helped her feel more confident in making her request.

We practiced how she would ask for the number she wanted. She practiced saying the number out loud without being embarrassed about it or turning red in the face, and she got used to the idea of making her case about her own value.

The day of the meeting, she was terrified, but she managed to ask for the number she wanted. She recounted to me that she blurted it out. I had told her to wait for a reaction, not to fill the air with her own chatter. She sat back and waited, and curbed her urge to explain any further why she deserved that number, even though it felt uncomfortable to sit through the awkward pause. She didn't get the exact number she wanted, but she got more money than they were initially going to give her. And more importantly, she learned how to negotiate in future discussions about salary. Over the next few positions she took, she was able to have money conversations more easily, though it took a lot of discomfort and awkward pauses.

Many years later I ran into her at a conference. She was tossing her head back, laughing at a "low" number a company had offered her—mid six figures. This was a number much higher than the one she was afraid of so long ago. It was amazing to see and hear what a difference a few years makes. It made an impression on me. Asking for your worth takes practice and time, and in the few short years that passed since my working with her, she went from fear to being so empowered that she knew when even a very high number was not worth her time or effort. I was delighted to see her laugh about it, to know that numbers weren't going to kill or define her. She could talk about them and exist with them with ease, and even with a smile.

*Everyone* is somewhat uncomfortable talking about money. Our culture doesn't encourage it, and yet makes it the ultimate form of success. A survey by Wells Fargo found that Americans are more uncomfortable talking about personal finances than about politics, religion, and even death. The survey also found a gender difference. "Half of women (50 percent) find it difficult talking with others about personal finances, versus 38 percent of men." Another poll found that younger Americans are starting to change the etiquette around money conversations, and that they "are more open about discussing credit scores and income levels in a dinner party setting than any other generation." The bottom line is that we all need to be talking about money more.

When people are nervous about salary negotiations, I also talk to them about who is in control of the money that they want. It's a way of reframing this situation and conversation. This is to say that while you're uncomfortable, your boss is likely uncomfortable, too. A bit of context when you're asking for that money: The request has to get to the person in charge of the money and that is likely not the person you're talking to directly. The request will have to be cleared at several different levels. It helps to know that the person on the other side of the table also doesn't really enjoy having this conversation. Expressing empathy for the situation—"I know neither of us really wants to be having this conversation"—can help alleviate tension and work in your favor.

Basic salary negotiations tell you to ask others what they make and do market research. Asking friends and colleagues if they are open to discussing salaries is great. But when it comes to Bragging Better, the focus should be on laying out your work and arguing for better compensation, regardless of what others are being paid. Yes, your ask should be based on market research, but your ask will also be unique to the value you bring to the table. As I've said, I believe that Bragging Better requires that we help other people rise, but it's difficult to do that if we can't even help ourselves. This is especially difficult for women and people of color. Inequality around money is a whole other book, but it needs to be acknowledged.

You are almost never looking at the money a business brings in unless you're running it. I do run my own business, so I'm equipped to talk about the numbers while pitching my business and my services all day. This is one reason why salary negotiations are difficult, not to mention the fact that you're not talking about money very often in your job, and not as it relates to your company as a whole. Unless you're in finance or you're in a position to be working with a company's finances, which is a small population, it's going to be hard to talk about money and to negotiate because you don't do it often. Again, you shouldn't just "know" how to do these things; you don't have good models, and everyone is hush-hush about money because it's a personal and taboo topic, but it's one that needs to be brought into the open. Negotiation takes a lot of practice.

In a negotiation, you are also allowed to take a step back, which a lot of people don't realize. You are allowed to think about an offer and take your time in answering. There is a tremendous amount of power in silence or thought, and sometimes that can be used to your advantage by making someone else uncomfortable. Letting something hang in the air, or sleeping on it overnight, is fine. You don't have to answer right away, even if the reason is you just don't want to.

A few examples of things you can say:

- "I need to think about it and I'll get back to you."
- "I'm going to sleep on it and follow up with you tomorrow."
- "Can we pause this, retreat, and come back to it next week?"
- "I'm thinking this over. Can we schedule a time to follow up?"

When you enter your negotiation, be prepared to use numbers. If you can share a brag like, "I brought in [X] amount of new sales, so I am actively looking out for the company's interests and making money for the brand," you'll be making a powerful statement in a negotiation. It's one thing to do your market research, but it's another to show in dollars what you're actually bringing to the table. Your boss will be considering you as a whole package—how well you work with others, how you interact with clients, your decorum and overall workplace behavior. But the most important factor is often the amount of money flowing in as a direct result of your presence, so don't be afraid to throw out numbers. Numbers are hard to argue with. If you can show that you're making them more money than they're paying you for, they have an excellent reason to pay you more.

Something I tell lots of people: Salary negotiations are often not personal—they are business decisions. That's what I remind people of when they get nervous about the negotiation. The most powerful thing you can do in a salary negotiation is to stick to facts and lean away from emotion. The person on the other side of the table is making a business decision. I don't want to sound ruthless, but it's true. They are trying to get the best talent for the least amount of money. Why would they want to overpay? Why would they not try to get a deal?

I was negotiating pay with someone I wanted to work with who was above my budget for the project. She framed it in a way that made me see that I would lose money if I didn't hire her. She showed me all the ways in which she could help me expand my writing and get me more paid speaking gigs. I realized that I literally couldn't afford to lose her. Obviously, you can guess that I hired her.

But perhaps even more important than what you say is

the confidence with which you make your ask. Take a cue from top executive and TEDWomen cofounder Pat Mitchell, who, after recalling a salary negotiation gone bad, noted: to "be prepared to present yourself for a raise or promotion, or a seat on a board, or whatever it is," your stance has to be "'I am qualified to make this ask. I am right.'"

# 10

# Public Speaking

Public speaking has become an industry that is highly competitive and highly profitable. It's a huge piece of public relations, company visibility, and your own career trajectory. There is no better current brag than a speaking gig. It allows for you to present yourself and your work, interact with others on a panel, showcase your persona in real time, as well as tout your ability to hold a strong interactive Q&A portion. There are more speaking opportunities than ever before. But the space is more crowded than ever before, too.

Many career paths are amplified by being on a stage. Watching someone on a stage makes you respect them more, because someone has seen fit to give them the microphone. Someone else has decided their message is worthy. Showing your work on a grand scale to the general public is a way of validating what you do and gaining the title of thought leader in your field. This works across industries, from tech to media, science to the arts. Speaking is a way of taking your message to a big stage and showing everyone what you've got. The benefits are significant, from visibility to more money, respect within the industry, and the opportunity to rub shoulders with contemporaries and other notable professionals.

Clients constantly come to me asking whether or not I book speaking gigs before they ask to be placed in the *New York Times*. This is because giving speeches and participating on panels are often quicker ways to Brag Better now than waiting to be covered in a press outlet.

In a Harris Poll commissioned by Prezi, 70 percent of people who *do* give presentations describe presenting as a critical factor in their overall career success. Warren Buffett, speaking to business students at Columbia University in 2009, touted the importance of public speaking. "You can improve your value by 50 percent just by learning communication skills—public speaking."

There are a lot of ways your Campaign of You needs to approach speaking. The first is to ask yourself where you want to speak and to cull a list of your targeted speaking gigs. Ask yourself why you'd like to speak at each of these events and how each particular gig will further your goals. Then, using what you've learned about pitching, target conference organizers and those in charge. Speaking events, particularly large ones, are booked at least six months ahead of time, so pitching someone on being a speaker a month beforehand won't work. Your best bet is to start early and assume you will be booked for the following year if they bite.

## The Brag Breakdown with Susan Cain: Get into Public Speaking (Even When You'd Rather Die)

*Susan Cain wrote the best-selling book* Quiet: The Power of Introverts in a World That Can't Stop Talking. *Since* Quiet *came out in 2012, Cain has launched Quiet Revolution, a business centered on helping introverts shine in the office. As an introvert herself, she found public speaking terrifying—but Cain knew it was important. Here is how she got through her fear.*

### The Impact Is Worth Overcoming the Fear

"I famously had such a public speaking phobia when I first started all this, [and] I really had to overcome [it]. Once I did that, I've actually been really struck by the by-product of it. Giving a talk has such a disproportionate impact in terms of how much people then listen to what you have to say."

### Speaking Is the Shortcut to Getting Your Message Out

"You could spend hundreds of hours getting a message out by writing a memo, or you could spend five minutes up on a stage. You'll have more impact from those five minutes on the stage. There's something about expressing yourself from a podium that causes you to be regarded as an authority in your field. The impact you can have that way is enormous."

### Remember You're in Control

"You're the one who's in charge of what happens on that stage. So, it's your message [and] your way of delivering the message."

**Face Your Fear in Small Doses**

"If [you] feel like [you] have some kind of message to share, it's worth staring down that fear. The key is to do it in very small chunks to expose yourself to it—to the fear—until you contain it."

## Where Do I Place You?

When you build your Campaign of You, you have to refine your lane, message, and tone to be successful. Speaking opportunities are refinement on steroids. This means you have to know exactly where in a conference's programming you would fall and exactly who you'll be speaking in front of, and you need to get as specific as possible. When I changed my focus from PR to the more nuanced concept of how to Brag Better and train leadership, nobody could really tell where to put me: Did I fit in with the personal branding specialists? A media panel? A PR panel? As a result, I didn't get a lot of speaking gigs. Once I really refined the Brag Better message, tightened my focus, and communicated where and how I would fit into a conference, it began to click and I got more gigs.

## "I Want to Be Booked"

Many of my clients and friends want to speak more often, but they leave out one crucial piece: that they are open to being booked and available, anywhere. You should almost have a sign on your back. (I do, it's a denim jacket with "Brag Better" embroidered on it. Taking my own premise seriously!)

You have to *tell people you want to be booked. Directly.* I have had many clients that want to give speeches, but nowhere on their personal sites or bios do they talk about previous speaking gigs or provide a booking email or speaking agent contact. That is one of the biggest barriers to getting talks. You must ask for gigs and/or show, from photo evidence or listings, that you are available for them. It's as simple as that. But everyone leaves it out. By making sure to have photos of your past speaking engagements and having a tab on your personal site with information on how to book you to speak, you change that perception for a conference booker or speaking agent. Plus, you show you're available to do it, and that you want to. Say so.

## Tips for Speaking Success

The mark of a good panel or talk is feeling like you were a success, but also that you left the audience more informed and better off than when you began. (For me, success is also wearing a great outfit and feeling like I got some good laughs. I also usually feel a wave of relief and eat a cookie. All markers of success.)

The business marker of speaking success is getting booked again and, even better, having audience members come up to you and ask for your card so they can book you to speak. Make it clear you want to speak again in those interactions, or *even tell them while you're on stage.* Thank the audience and tell them they can book you, too. Be bold. A successful speech also assures the organizers that they got what they wanted, paid for, and most importantly, expected.

Here is a list of questions that I have asked conference organizers in the past in order to prepare my message and presentation. It's important to know the answers to as many of these questions as possible before you go onstage, so that you can rock it.

- What would make this a success for you?
- What does the audience expect to hear?
- How large is the audience?
- How large is the room, and can you share a picture?
- Will I be standing or sitting?
- How will the seating be arranged?
- Can I see the lighting arrangement?
- Is someone introducing me?
- Will this be photographed or taped?
- How many panelists are there?
- Who is moderating?
- Can I get a sense of the questions beforehand?

When I used to be really scared about giving talks, these questions helped ease the knots in my stomach. So did cookies—again, a universal salve. But for some reason, seeing photos of the actual room I was speaking in made me feel the most comfortable. The more unknowns I could remove, the better.

Be sure to talk to audience members after your speech, too. I've gotten many clients, not just speaking gigs, from people who have attended my talks. Plus, it's really fun to interact with the audience and hear the questions they have. I always make sure to leave time for a Q&A at the end of every talk so that people can ask me their specific grievances. Bragging Better is so personal and different for everyone that I want my audiences to feel seen and heard.

Talking to the audience after your gig also reinforces for you how good you are at your job. You might hear questions or perspectives you've never heard before. You might also hear stories of deep vulnerability. It's amazing what people will say to you when they believe you are an authority. I am constantly bowled over by questions, particularly from young women, around more intimate parts of their careers and aspirations. I feel so lucky that I get to tell them to go for it. It's a responsibility, but one I cherish.

My most memorable interaction thus far was with a young woman who approached me after a speech I gave. She was visibly nervous. She asked me if "her dreams were too big" because "everyone in my town thinks they are and tells me so." My heart shattered into a million pieces. It was at that moment that I realized how much bigger this was than raising your hand or talking about what you've done. It was also about being allowed to dream. I told her to screw all those people and what they think, and that nobody's dreams are too big if you work hard and go after it. Part of this book is for her.

I've learned more about what I do from what others ask me, and I'd bet you will, too. Questions often differ from what you think audience members want to hear, because you're simply making an educated guess. You can learn so much from your audience! Ask them questions, too.

## The Brag Breakdown with David Rubenstein: On Persuasion

*David Rubenstein, prominent philanthropist, investor, and businessman, is no stranger to being in public. He understands the persuasive power of speaking up. Here he shares his tips for getting people to listen.*

**Once You Have Their Attention, Make Them Feel Good**

"Take John F. Kennedy's inaugural address, Martin Luther King' Jr's 'I Have a Dream' speech, and Abraham Lincoln's Gettysburg address. What do they have in common? They were brief. They never said a specific thing that they were going to do. They ended with the word 'God,' or [something] more or less in that sense. They left people without specifics but a sense of a greater purpose. [They left their audience] feeling better for having heard the speech. That's what I try to do. . . . I try to give a speech that makes people feel good."

**Find Their Motivation**

"All of life is about persuading people. The best way to persuade people to do what you want is to know what motivates them. When I meet people, I ask them a lot of questions: about their background, what makes them tick, what motivates them. Ask questions and you'll be able to discern a lot about them."

**Build Your Connection**

"You'll inevitably find something there—a connection. The more you talk about it, it connects you more and, therefore, you have something in common. And once you have something in common, people are more likely to listen to you."

## Sharing the Stage

A few years ago, I was part of a panel with the largest audience I'd ever spoken to—nearly two thousand people. It was terrifying. I was prepared, had prepped myself by reading answers to tons of questions, and was wearing a favorite red jumpsuit. But I royally messed up: I went in with the attitude that I wanted to "win" and be the "favorite" panelist. Instead of realizing the opportunity to bond with my fellow panelists and join forces, I alienated myself and came off like a jerk. This is not what audiences want to see. It was embarrassing. By making it into a competition, I did the entire audience and myself a disservice.

Like much of Bragging Better, being a successful speaker doesn't require that you "win" or be the "best." When on a panel, your colleagues are there to create a great conversation, help one another, and help an audience. Read up on your fellow panelists, consider their work, and compliment them. Create good bonding energy. There is room enough for everyone to Brag Better on a panel. While you can't always expect the same of everyone else, you can lead by example. Again, a crucial part of Bragging Better is helping bolster the voices of others. Check yourself. Everyone shining together is a real win.

## The Ultimate Stage: Television Appearances

Television is the hardest press hit to secure, and the most difficult to succeed at. It's also often the most exciting, nerve-racking, and biggest opportunity to get visibility quickly, like with Nina back in Chapter 1.

The upsides of going on TV are enormous, and sometimes they let you sit in the green room, which means you get free snacks. An audience can experience you fully. If you have a TV clip that makes its way around online, you can use it to get more TV and to pitch articles, panels, and speeches. It can double your speaking fees and it usually puts you next to someone who viewers know. If you're sitting next to Katie Couric, for example, it means you are worth listening to and watching. You receive validation from someone who a lot of people look to. It's a visual endorsement.

TV is so hard to crack because it's a giant funnel, and there are a lot of people trying to wedge themselves into that funnel because they, too, want to get on air. There are so many proposed segments and only so much time. We live in the era of the warp-speed, twenty-four-hour news cycle. It's also a fickle beast. Sometimes I've booked clients who have gotten bumped or moved to a new hour or taken off entirely due to last-minute breaking news or a quick change in the script. It's unpredictable.

You can prepare and practice with TV, but success comes with appearing over and over again if you are able to. This is why the best preparation is getting on camera anywhere at any time, including online streaming TV (nothing to sniff at—people do it all the time). The most important thing is to gain clips. It's much easier to pitch for television when you have a previous appearance to show, which also conveys that at some point someone booked you and made the call to put you on their show, even if it's a small one.

Breaking through for television and getting into rotation (an expert or source that is in the arsenal of people producers call upon) is the toughest part. It's often a long and arduous process. Don't be discouraged. A lot of this has to do with the fact that a producer can rarely take a gamble on a guest. You can't suck, or it makes for bad TV. Producers are worried about how you appear (particularly, and unfairly, if you're a woman), how you sound, and how viewers will react to you. They need to be sure you're going to do well, often because the show is live. If you go silent on live TV, there is no escape.

This just means you have to step it all the way up when getting on the air.

## When to Not Brag

Bragging Better isn't about bragging all the time. You don't want to tire an audience. nor do you want to tire yourself. Understanding when to pull back is an important skill. Sometimes you need to make the decision to be private with your work. Especially if this is a new skill for you, you're gonna get pooped sometimes. I do, too. The good news is as a member of The Qualified Quiet, sitting back and taking it in isn't foreign to you.

I coached a client who was sick of being on a plane two hundred days a year, giving lots of speeches. She said she was over it. The first photo of her everywhere—her headshot, the photo on the landing page of her personal website—showed her with a microphone on a large stage in front of a large audience. That communicates "I want to speak, pay me to speak, it's a huge part of my business." In order to change that perception, she needed to convey a different message, change the photos, and change her offerings. It's up to you to put boundaries around your public life. Not all Bragging Better is good; it's only good if it serves your larger purpose.

### WHEN BRAGGING ISN'T EFFECTIVE

#### *You're Tired*

Understanding when to be quiet, or to listen, is a skill you likely already have as a member of The Qualified Quiet. Your quietness is part of who you are and can be quite powerful. You don't need to comment on every story or every scenario. The trick is to learn to strategically brag, not constantly brag.

After I give a speech or spend a lot of time doing a big project with lots of other people, I am completely depleted. I want to crawl into a hole and watch TV until my eyes pop out of my head and eat snacks and pet my dog. I know being around people, doing talks, and going to lots of meetings leaves me extremely tired. Know what your limits are and don't be afraid to enforce them. Sometimes it can be scary to turn down an opportunity for visibility, but if it's not going to serve your best interests and you're not going to kill it, there's no point in doing it. An audience can tell when your battery is running low.

### *You Need to Read the Room*

Sometimes it's just not the place and time to Brag Better. The focus shouldn't be only on you, and that's important to discern. Sometimes other people want to talk about themselves, and you'll get farther by letting them do it.

### *People Are Already Convinced*

There's a popular phrase that says "stop selling," which means you've already sold me; we don't need to hear any more. I used to be guilty of this. I'd get so excited or passionate that I didn't know when to stop. You're going to have to test the line, but if you can tell from people's faces or you're hearing "we get it" or "we hear you," then pump the brakes.

# 11

# Bragging Online

We have gone over a lot of in-real-life scenarios for Bragging Better, or scenarios where you have an audience of one or a few people. Now it's time to consider how we brag online. The landscape for sharing ourselves on the internet is vast and differs widely, from blogs to company websites to social media. But it's worth taking a moment to consider these audiences, which tend to be full of strangers.

## Social Media

Social media changes on a dime. "Likes" or metrics change, but a lot of the tactics and goals remain the same: to be proud, loud, and strategic. To communicate who you are and what you want and make it easy for people to help you. Your message needs to be consistent. That's what helps you grow, communicate, and Brag Better. And that's what helps you feel good sharing your work and contributions.

Social media is incredibly fickle. I tell clients to pick one platform you hate the least and do that one well. It beats doing all of them poorly (though of course you should have all the handles reserved just in case you decide to use them). Consider the medium—images for Instagram, hashtags for Twitter, for example.

When using hashtags, don't go overboard. Use no more than three so as not to look deranged. The most important part of sharing on social media isn't making sure all of your hashtags are perfect. Instead, your focus should be on using your chosen adjectives to best present yourself, deciding what audience you're going after and experiencing the sheer enjoyment of it. I love sharing memes on Instagram, and I love endless baby animals. Is it totally all things Brag Better all the time? No. Does it make me happy and communicate joy to share cute animals with those flipping through my stories? Yes. So I continue to do it.

Using social media is a choice. And when you choose to utilize social media outlets for your goals instead of simply for socializing, your shares can make a tremendous difference to your career. Comedians like Rob Delaney or Megan Amram, for example, wouldn't have the careers they do if it weren't for the bump they got with Twitter. Butts wouldn't be nearly as popular without Instagram (though I suspect butts were likely always popular). And some of those butts drive entire businesses. The point is, you can see careers that are made from users sharing work, like art and photos, from saavy social media posters. Yes, the internet can be a garbage fire of hatred, misogyny, and racism, but you can also find and create positive corners for your people to read, enjoy, and share.

## Keep Introducing Yourself Online

Online, you should be introducing yourself all the time. Consider an introductory post in each medium at least once a month. Something like, "In case you're new here, here is a link to my personal site and more about what I do. I run a company called FinePoint, I write, and I teach people to brag." Every time I've done that, it's yielded a comment from someone already following me who was interested in the work. I hadn't given them the proper context before, or they just hadn't seen it.

This means you have to repeat yourself a lot, but it's only repetitive to you. I think to myself, "How on *earth* could someone not know that I teach people to brag and self-promote?" Inevitably, they don't. Remember that many people haven't seen your past content. They might be new to following you, or they might not have been paying attention because it wasn't relevant to them at the time. After all, there are a lot of cute animals to look at on the internet. But as soon as they need help doing whatever it is you offer (or know someone else who needs help), they will take an interest in your work.

There are always more eyeballs to be had, and more people to win over. This means there is endless opportunity. It also means there is endless work to be done. You will never hit every person online with any one post. Just stay consistent, and people will eventually see your message.

### CAMPAIGN OF YOU ACTION LIST

- Revise your résumé.
  - Accurately list your previous work history.

  - Describe what you did with positive, strong language.
  - List your awards and accomplishments.
- Revise or write your bios.
  - Create a long, short, and two-line bio. (The long bio is one page, including everything; the short bio is a paragraph; and the two-line bio is two sentences.)
  - Remove hobbies, playful references, and creative titles.
  - Include hyperlinks.
  - Don't use weak verbs or passive voice.
  - Use your last name, not your first.
  - Include calls to action.
- Buy the domain of your name. (Grab all matching social media handles, even ones you don't think you'll use.)
- Build a basic website using an easy-to-use platform.
- Check your Google search results, and record what comes up on the first three pages.
- Set a Google alert for your name.
- Create a you@yourname.com email address.
- Review your email signature. (Make sure that it has the proper contact information.)
- Choose three different types of people or audiences and craft an introduction for yourself for each.
- Practice introducing yourself to someone above you.
- Practice introducing yourself to a coworker friend.
- Craft a pitch document for yourself. (This pitch document will contain three to four angles for your story and Campaign of You. Begin with a central and more general pitch. Then break it down into three or four different audiences.)
  - Write your pitch for a potential journalist or writer.

  - Write your pitch for a conference or TV booker.
  - Write your pitch for a potential client.
  - Write your pitch for someone you admire.
- Make sure your headshots are up-to-date and communicate what you want.
  - Get a new headshot every year, and more often if you change your appearance.
  - Use the same headshot everywhere.
- Get new business cards or order more.
- Make a list of dream panels and places you want to speak.
  - Organize them by the time of year if they happen annually.
  - Begin drafting your pitches to conference organizers or bookers, and figure out their contact information.
- Gather clips for your speaker reel, if you have them.
  - Make one for speaking gigs and one for television appearances.
  - Include the highlights of your public appearances to serve as the ultimate quick brag—a reel shouldn't be more than a few minutes long.
- Make it clear you want to get booked by explicitly telling people on your personal site, social media, or email signature. (You can also create a separate email, like speaking@yourname.com.)
- Bonus Points: Write your core speech.
  - Create a twenty-minute version.
  - Create a forty-minute version.

## Part 3

# GOING PRO

We've covered the core tenets—being proud, loud, and strategic. I've given you a playbook from my own work as a publicist, and now you know how to begin your Campaign of You. You're fully equipped to think about the nuts and bolts of Bragging Better. The final act is about what it means to be in public, how to prepare yourself for the inevitable ups and downs of visibility, and how you can share what you've learned with the world, your network, and your friends.

# 12

# Facing Your Bragging Fears

About a decade ago, I had one of my first assignments for a major business publication. I had pitched the editor for months and finally secured a column. When I got the assignment, I was so excited that I furiously jotted notes in my phone and on a random phone bill that was within my reach. I spent weeks crafting the eight-hundred-word essay, emailing friends for feedback on my drafts, and repeatedly thinking it was absolute garbage or maybe great (this is how writing goes). I tinkered with the headline and probably wrote about one hundred different opening paragraphs.

I submitted the article for publication, and I remember the thrill of seeing it posted. My name! On the internet! On a site with a big name! I was still unable to believe that this award-winning outlet wanted writing from my voice. As soon as the shock wore off, I wanted immediate validation from strangers on the internet, so I went to the absolute worst place to do so: the comments section.

In less than one hour, a comment appeared. "I'm sure this person is going to tell me to be on the cover of *Vogue*, and just how amazing my writing is and that my hair is shiny," I thought. As you can maybe guess, that did not happen. It said, "I want that two minutes of my life back." And I remember it clear as day, ten years later.

I know now: Never read the comments. I have a key chain with my mail key on it that literally says "Never Read the Comments." The comments sections of articles bring out the worst in people. Flippant, nasty comments that would make you blush and even cry are whipped off by readers hiding behind their screens.

This experience taught me a valuable lesson, in addition to not touching the cesspool of the comments section. It's very difficult, scary, and sometimes hurtful to put yourself out there. Whether it's on a stage or in a meeting, the willingness to speak up, assert an opinion, and shine a light on yourself and your work means that others will have something to say about it.

I've been hurt a lot, but I've dusted myself off and gotten back up. So has anyone else in a public position. It's part of the territory. The juice is worth the squeeze. If you stay grounded and learn to roll with it, the experience is an overall net positive, or else I wouldn't be here writing this book.

Your fears are normal. So normal that this is what I help people do, day in and day out.

Being afraid of what people will think and say is the most common fear I encounter with clients. Who wouldn't have that fear? When you decide to put yourself in front of an audience of one or ten thousand, people are going to have opinions about you and your words. It's only natural to be anxious about what others will say. I'm anxious of what you're saying about this book! Right now! I hope you're loving it.

## You're More in Control Than You Think

My guess is that you already know that and you are reading this book to figure out how to step out into the spotlight and not feel like you want to run and hide. One of the biggest concerns I hear, from college students to corporate board members, is "What if I get hurt by being in public?"

You have a greater ability to foresee the future than you think. You don't have a crystal ball, but these strategies help you mitigate potential risk. And you still might get burned a little. But you'll be okay once you take a step back and learn from the hard lessons.

A few years ago, a young woman emailed me to tell me that because of an article I wrote, she felt confident enough to begin pitching her writing. She told me she was scared—as a young college student, she was worried that no editor would take her seriously. So I gave her some advice, similar to what I have written here about the power of a good pitch. I sent it to her and she did it. And as a result, after multiple attempts she got her first piece published. When I get messages like this, I feel so grateful and extremely proud. These messages make the anxiety and fear worth it. I emailed her back to tell her that she was a badass for even trying in the first place. You're a badass for trying. You get points for that.

This chapter will prepare you for potential blowback and criticism, but it will also help you feel okay making people mad. By the end of it, you'll be more comfortable starting conversations and be proud to be you. If the results of putting yourself out there were all bad, and didn't result in opportunities for new business, press, or career gains, then I wouldn't be nudging you out there in the first place.

## What's Your Nightmare Question?

I do an exercise with clients called Nightmare Question. I'm referring to the creepy-crawly question that nags at us in the middle of the night. We identify the deepest, darkest question a journalist or conference audience member could ask. And then we answer it. I know you can do this exercise, too. Once you take a swing at that big scary "boo," it usually helps you face the fear, even if it's uncomfortable.

For most of my clients, addressing their Nightmare Question means confronting deep fears of inadequacy or a lack of feeling qualified. The point of the Nightmare Question is to prepare for the worst-case scenario, but also to shine a light on a question that will *never be asked of you*. I want you to think of the worst thing that you could possibly be asked. What's that one thing in the back of your head that you ask or say to yourself when you're down? Yeah, that awful, nasty, completely unwarranted and irrational question. That one. I want you to bring it into the light and tell it to scram—by crafting a strong rebuttal.

For me, my Nightmare Question is, "Who do you think you are? There are so many other millennial entrepreneurs that are more successful than you." This question highlights my fear that my work isn't good enough, or that everyone is going to think I'm a total joke. It also creeps up on me when I'm feeling bad, or scared, or unsuccessful. When I shine a light on it, I think, "Okay, I can handle that." My response to this question is, "I feel lucky and grateful. I try my hardest to put out a good work product. I'm proud of what I've done. I've written two books, published hundreds of articles, and trained hundreds of clients." At least now I have an answer to the question that will *never, ever, ever again ever, be asked of me.*

Shine the light on your Nightmare Question and then get ready to answer that little voice in your head. Why do I have you answering a question that I promise will never be asked of you? Because preparedness makes you feel better. And you will never have to use it, but you have something to shout back into the dark.

These questions are reflections of your own insecurities. They are deep and dark. The exercise is designed to help you call the monster out from the closet, invite him to sit next to you, and tell him you're not afraid of him anymore. Preparing an answer makes him disappear. That's the thing about nightmares—they're not real, but they do feel very real.

Some example Nightmare Questions from clients:

- "You had the help of family money and have done nothing yourself, have you?"
- "How are you going to succeed with your track record?"
- "Why would anyone want to be your business partner considering how you have worked with others in the past?"
- "Have you considered that your product isn't receiving funding because it's just a bad idea?"

Now, let's craft your answer. When I do this process with people, I pose the question to them and make them answer it. I then help them pinpoint their specific fear and address that. I'll show you how this works with my Nightmare Question.

Again, the question is, "Who do you think you are? There are so many other millennial entrepreneurs that are more successful than you."

First, I break down why this is in my head: Working for myself is hard and just having the confidence to continue to fight for your own job can be trying. When I feel like really being a jerk to myself, I do the really lovely thing of comparing myself to people who are more "successful" than I am. As we know, this is a completely useless exercise. Now I know where the question originates.

The next step is to imagine this question being asked of me, say, on a panel. Note: If anyone asked me this on a panel, it would be completely deranged. But I still fear it. Fear is not rational. In order to slay this dragon I need to continue with the exercise. I think about how I'd react. I imagine myself sitting up straight and speaking with a consistent tone, while also wanting to burst into tears. I think about the Brag Better key components, and I first go with gratitude. I acknowledge that I am lucky to be in the situation I am. I then lead with pride—that I work hard to the best of my ability. Don't just take that nagging voice seriously—prove it wrong.

To be clear: I have never, ever had anyone ask a client of mine their specific Nightmare Question. I don't think anyone ever will. I used to bet each of my clients that if their Nightmare Question were ever asked of them, I'd give them a hundred dollars. My publisher will not let me extend this offer to you, dear reader, but if someone ever asks you your Nightmare Question, I will send you a refund for this book.

Here are some answers to the example Nightmare Questions:

**"You had the help of family money and have done nothing yourself, have you?"**

"Listen, I'm not going to pretend I haven't been incredibly fortunate. My dad is someone who I deeply admire" (whether you like him or not). "I'm not sure I could measure up to his level of work, but I certainly am willing to try."

**"How are you going to succeed with your track record?"**

"I may have taken big swings and missed—risk is inherently risky—but I'm still at bat. I'm still willing to try again and again and again. Plus, I've learned a lot from my failures. I view them as learning experiences. I've learned how to raise money, I've learned how to hire people, I've learned how to manage people, and I think that no company lasts forever."

Or

"Nothing lasts forever, but I'm still here willing to take more swings, and I have a depth of experience that a first-time founder would not."

Or

"You learn more from your fuckups than you do from your successes, so I've earned a lot of knowledge."

**"Why would anyone want to be your business partner considering how you have worked with others in the past?"**

"Listen, working with anyone is very difficult. I've spent a lot of time thinking about this, and managing a partnership is really, really hard. If I ever do end up having a business partner again, I will have to look at the past and what I've done in those relationships to create negative environments or create hostility, and that's just something I don't want going forward."

**"Have you considered that your product isn't receiving funding because it's just a bad idea?"**

"Well, I don't think it's a bad idea, and I don't really appreciate that judgment. There are a lot of amazing ideas and products being funded right now, and people are always looking for novel ideas to support with their investment. I'm going to continue looking for the right fit, and I know that the right person is out there who will believe in the idea."

Or

"I've spent a long time fund-raising and realizing that a lot of it is a total crapshoot, a lot of it is deeply biased, and I'm learning to refine my deck every single time. I believe in the product, and I believe that there's still a funder out there."

## Fear Is Normal

It's okay to be scared. Everyone is scared, all the time. Humans are made of 98 percent water, so we are essentially cucumbers filled with anxiety (this is not my joke, but one I love), just walking around with our own scary, sad thoughts. I was on the phone with a megastar—at least in the business world—and she was terrified to give her upcoming TED Talk. (She had already done one before, so, um, what did she have to be worried about?) She was practicing for *four hours a day*. I reminded myself that if this person was nervous, everyone must get nervous.

Choosing to Brag Better, whether it's raising a hand among colleagues or giving a speech, is a tremendous expression of vulnerability with uncertain results. I'm proud of you for choosing to do it anyway. Seeing and choosing to do a hard thing despite fear is growth, and it's awesome. Give yourself a pat on the back for even stepping up to the plate.

The keys are control, preparedness, a feeling that we're all in it together, and some hard work.

## Dissent Is Powerful

I don't blame The Qualified Quiet for not bragging. You see the heat and the hate, and you don't want to participate. However, disagreement—not hate speech, but people simply not agreeing with you, even in a nasty way—is actually a marker of success. I was so excited when my podcast on resale fashion (*It Never Gets Old*) got its first mean review! I know that sounds strange, but that means people who aren't just supporters of mine are listening to it. These were real strangers who cared enough to post a comment, even if they didn't like it and logged on just to say so.

If everyone agrees with you, you likely don't have a wide enough audience. Debate can be constructive and important in disseminating your message. Look at these new points of view that expand your message or vice versa. Know the difference between new points of view that can help you expand your message and the garbage fire that is the internet.

After my past experience with the mean comments, I learned to ask friends and colleagues to sift through my writing for constructive and kind criticism. This doesn't mean to tune out all feedback that isn't 100 percent glowing and positive. Constructive criticism can help you grow, change, and get better. Nasty, non-constructive noise won't.

In this day and age of echo chambers, not everyone *should* agree with you. You don't want an audience of only yes-women. As Luvvie Ajayi points out: "Approaching the world with the idea that I want people to agree with me is actually a trap. [Having] everyone love who I am is the quickest way to do nothing that is real, nothing that you're supposed to do, and nothing that is actually gonna make an impact." That's a powerful perspective shift, one you could even choose to see as a responsibility or mission statement. As Ajayi says, "I always tell people that your job is not for people to agree with you or think that you're some magical fairy being. Your job is not to avoid criticism. Your job is to be *true*. You have to be prepared for criticism and people who are not going to like what you're gonna say."

Dissent means you've broken out of the echo chamber. Neither one is particularly fun, obviously, but experiencing dissent and criticism means you're getting past a closed loop, that you actually have reach. And reach is the door that opens opportunity for you.

"When nobody is critiquing you," Ajayi says, "you're probably doing or saying nothing of note." Doing work that's worthy of attention, worthy of bragging, will likely come with a side of criticism—that's the reality of our world, personal or professional, physical or online. By calculating the odds and determining the best way to put your message and presence into the world, you minimize as much risk as possible. Front-ending this work and preparing for all scenarios, understanding what could happen, and learning how to tune out what is simple, unproductive anxiety results in a more effective message, and an output that is true to you with your best interests in mind.

## Feeling the Backlash

Bragging sometimes doesn't win you friends. This can be particularly true at the office, where there is a ton of politics. You're dealing with a lot of egos, opinions, insecurities, someone stealing your yogurt from the fridge, and feelings, all day, every day. It's really hard to navigate, and sometimes you can get some backlash for Bragging Better.

## THE PEEVED COWORKERS

A common example I see is peeved coworkers whose low self-esteem is wounded by your bragging. This stems not from your issues, but from theirs. However, you have to work with them. Handle this by having a conversation with or confronting them in a way that doesn't make them even more defensive. If he or she is determined to just be salty about your touting your accomplishments, let it be. But also know that that person might have adverse reactions in the future.

The first thing to figure out is how much of the problem is you and how much of it is them. Bragging will make people uncomfortable and anxious because they can't do it themselves. It will make people mad at first, because they see it and feel there's no way they can do it.

You are not responsible for other people's feelings. But, you have to work with these people, so it depends on what their resistance looks like. Pull them aside for a one-on-one conversation. Say something like, "I just want to make sure there aren't any roadblocks to us getting this project done. If there's an issue you can always come to me to discuss it." If you feel that the person doesn't want to have a conversation, but you want to resolve the issue, you can say, "You can always write me a note. It would be great for us to have a conversation, but whatever works for you."

What if someone is blunt with you? What if you have a friend or colleague who says, "Yeah, to be honest, I don't like your bragging." You can respond by saying, "Cool, I'm sorry you don't like the bragging, but I want to make sure that I'm being heard and that my contributions are being acknowledged. You can brag, too, you know." Another way you can put it is, "Hey, I'm working really hard to be heard, and I'm not open to feedback at this time."

If you hear through the grapevine that someone doesn't like your bragging, you can simply ignore it. If you feel the need to, you can respond to the person who tells you with, "Honestly, that's not really helpful. You don't need to tell me anything like that ever again." Respond only to those who address you directly.

If you hear negative bragging feedback from a boss or employer, you might say, "I want to be a good employee. Can you get more specific with that feedback?" If you hear back, "Oh, in meetings sometimes you talk over people," you can say, "Thanks for that feedback. I will take note of it." A boss might say, "Well, we already know what you've accomplished," and you can say, "That's really great. What's the best way for me to continue to communicate that to you in a way that works for you?"

As you are communicating, consider how much power and control this person has over you, and how much your bragging highlights their own resistance. If you're dealing with someone you have to report to directly and they're in charge of your whole work life, then you do have to deal with their feelings on the matter. Sometimes you're just going to have to tiptoe around someone's feelings with your bragging, and if that person controls how much you get paid or whether or not you get promoted, then you might have to brag less for a period of time.

If you're responding to someone else on your level, you can say, "Okay, thanks so much for the feedback," and then just move on.

### PROMOTION JEALOUSY

Another common blowback from Bragging Better is jealousy over a promotion. Maybe said irked colleague wanted that promotion herself. She may even feel that she is capable of doing the work required to get to that level. Tread carefully, but also make sure your promotion doesn't get outshined by everyone else's fears. In touchier scenarios, leading with gratitude is often best.

You shouldn't have to apologize for getting a promotion. If someone really has your best interests in mind, they'll be happy for you. People can hold two feelings at once. They can be angry they didn't get the promotion *and* they can be happy for their friend.

### HANDLING THE BACKLASH

Sometimes there's only so much you can do when your Bragging Better lights up jealousy and ill will from those around you. Be as polite and grateful as you can, but also make sure you address any of these issues with your colleagues. Ask them how they'd like to hear of your wins in the future, or if they have anything they'd like to talk about in an open, judgment-free space. In the end, don't drive yourself insane trying to manage others' feelings. It's just not your job, and it's not in the job description.

## Fear Is Real

Often our fear of being in public stems from the horror stories we hear from others. I want you to be protected to the best of your ability by helping you lay out solutions to these fears.

It's not a pretty picture, I'll admit: trolls, name-calling, and worse. This is especially true for women, people of color, and the LGBTQIA community—basically anyone who isn't a white man. The harassment, doxing (exposing of someone's personal information, like a home address), and social media mobs need to stop. It's important to be aware of the actual and serious risks.

"I've always been inclined to not be visible," admits filmmaker and writer dream hampton. She's always been aware of history—specifically, what history has shown happens to women, especially Black women, who make themselves visible, speak out, take action, or make an impact. And when they act against a powerful person or a powerful system? The reaction can be even scarier, something hampton knows all too well.

The blowback of entering the public discourse has shifted in the online age, hampton notes, particularly related to her executive production of the award-winning and explosive TV series *Surviving R. Kelly*: "To be targeted in this moment [means] being doxed [and] people being able to find your address." She shares that people have posted her private conversations and DMs, posted Photoshopped pictures of her, sent harassing tweets and messages, and targeted her young adult daughter. And as hampton learned, such targeting can often come from those you'd least expect. After hiring a cybersecurity officer to clean up the doxing and assess how she might also be at risk, hampton was informed that she was most likely to be targeted by Black men: "My main threat was random Black men. Which, as a heterosexual woman who has exclusively dated Black men, who loves Black people, that's fucking heartbreaking." Her advice? Brace for blowback, whether or not you expect it.

In a 2017 survey by Reclaim Your Domain, which asked

three thousand Americans about their experiences online, 47 percent said that they had experienced online harassment. Of those ages eighteen to twenty-nine, that figure skyrocketed to 65 percent. In the same study, 41 percent of women ages fifteen to twenty-nine said they censor themselves online because they worry about harassment. And twenty-one out of those three thousand people stopped using social media completely after being victims of online harassment. I think we can all agree that this number is much too high.

Many clients are afraid that they will be baited into a shouting match on TV. Or that their words will be sliced and diced into a sound bite, whether on TV or in the press, that makes them look awful. We are often at the mercy of producers and editors. Shock value, yelling, and extremism is what gets hits and clicks, so it can be easy to feel like you don't want to participate. It's easier than ever to be made to look bad or unreasonable. These fears are very real and substantiated. They deserve to be heard.

## EVERYTHING ELSE MEANT TO SCARE YOU INTO SILENCE

When women and "other" voices speak up, they are often met with a level of harassment and violence that's unfathomable. It's a very real fear. Scaring women and any other oppressed people into silence is a way of suppressing important messages. There are, unfortunately, a lot of examples of this.

Technology has a long way to go to solving online harassment. As long as people feel empowered to be cruel behind an anonymous screen, and face little to no consequences, they will continue to harass. There need to be better systems in place to combat and block these perpetrators. It can feel like a game of whack-a-mole with endless trolls popping up—the second you block one, more appear.

A *New Yorker* article states:

> According to a September Pew poll, a quarter of internet users have posted comments anonymously. As the age of a user decreases, his reluctance to link a real name with an online remark increases; 40 percent of people in the eighteen-to-twenty-nine-year-old demographic have posted anonymously. One of the most common critiques of online comments cites a disconnect between the commenter's identity and what he is saying, a phenomenon that the psychologist John Suler memorably termed the "online disinhibition effect." The theory is that the moment you shed your identity the usual constraints on your behavior go, too.

Our major social media companies are aware of these issues but are either ill-equipped or unwilling to step up. Don't be afraid of reporting someone on social media by hitting the "report abuse" button on Twitter or blocking anyone that is harassing you. I've done it before, and I will continue to do it when necessary. Keep your own logs and all receipts, if you're able. Filter all harassing messages to a folder for safekeeping in case, in the worst-case scenario, you need to use them. I'm sorry to say that you may have to prepare to deal with this.

## A "GOTCHA" MOMENT

Many clients are afraid that they will be caught in a "gotcha" situation, particularly on TV. This new type of ploy is a product of our time, a world of increasingly wacky reality shows and our short attention spans. They fear any kind of ambush or bait and switch. This can happen in more controversial fields like politics. However, for the most part, it is rare. If you're doing crisis work for an oil spill you're trying to cover up, then expect it. Otherwise, in 95 percent of the cases I've worked with, it's an irrational fear.

It is reasonable to be afraid of being baited into a shouting match. This is how many news shows raise their ratings. Higher ratings sell more advertising, which keeps shows on the air and media entities in business. That's how the system works. The system thrives on people punching each other, literally or figuratively, on TV.

I once booked a client for a TV spot. She ran a nonprofit surrounding women's reproductive health, which is a huge, crucial, hot-button issue. I pressed the TV producer to tell me exactly what the segment was about and who she would appear with on the air. It turned out that they planned to book her with her direct adversary to create conflict and, in their eyes, "good TV." I promptly pulled my client from the show. It wasn't productive for her and the organization. So, I killed it. I was pissed, but not surprised.

You can mitigate this result by asking a number of questions before the interview, particularly if it's on TV. We are often at the mercy of producers and editors, and when extremism is what gets clicks, it can be easy to not want to participate. It often means you should do it anyway, with a strong head on your shoulders to discern where and when your commentary is needed, and when you're just being used for ratings. In these cases, if it doesn't feel right, it isn't right.

Keep in mind that you never have to answer a question you don't want to. You can always say "No comment," "Let's move on to the next question," "Let's switch gears," "I'd prefer not to answer that," "Great question, but I'm not answering it at this time," or "Honestly, I need to think about that, so I'll get back to you."

You have more control than you think, and if you have to shut it down, that newsperson will change gears because they need to make good TV. You can also say, "I'm just going to have to say 'no comment' to that, and I'm sure you can understand why," while smiling, or, "I'm not going to speak on that at this time, but maybe down the road." Then you can redirect to whatever you want to talk about.

I will give you an extreme crisis PR scenario. This is a worst-case example, but it shows you that even in a contentious interview you can redirect. Use this to understand that even at a much lower or less controversial level, you are still in control.

Let's say that I am a VP of a technology company that is currently in trouble because of a data breach, and I'm going on TV to talk about our future technology predictions. The interviewer might say, "Well, you just had this huge data breach. Are you just doing this interview to cover your ass?" In that case, I could say, "I'm here to talk about our technology predictions for 2020 and how much we really care about the future of information. So let's stick to that topic." The interviewer might say, "Well, you're really sort of circling the issue here. You just exposed a bunch of user data and it really seems like sort of a cover-up." I could respond with, "Listen, as I said, I am here to talk about our predictions for 2020 and what we're really excited to do, what we're really excited to be a part of, so let's chat about it." It's rare that they would try a third time. And if they do, you can say "no comment," and then they will move on.

A lot of this comes with media training and the ability to finesse the moment, but you can easily have an eject button sentence ready. You are always in control of the conversation, and you can always redirect it to cover your talking points. Let's say you're really dying to talk about your book (I'll use *Brag Better* in this case), and the interviewer says, "Well, what do you think about the current political climate and how to navigate it?" You might respond with, "In a year like 2020, I believe that civic duty is partially talking about what you know. That's what my book is all about."

Just remember that you are in control, stick with your delivery, and redirect when necessary. Stay relaxed and don't get tense.

## BEING MADE TO LOOK BAD OR UNREASONABLE

Ask producers, or your interviewer, exactly how and where they are going to use your quotes and voice. Ask them if you get final say, or if they will show you what they're using ahead of time and consult with you. They likely won't do this, but it doesn't hurt to ask. Be sure to familiarize yourself with past work on these channels and with these outlets, especially with that writer or producer. If he or she has a history of more extreme stories, more outlandish segments, you need to do your homework and be forewarned. You can't go on *Jerry Springer* and expect *PBS NewsHour*.

## THE PEANUT GALLERY

The bottom line of Bragging Better is this: It's very easy to take a shot at someone who has decided to step out and put herself in public. Choosing to stand up and speak out makes you an easy target. The peanut gallery is everyone else judging you, talking about you, and even gossiping. You have zero control over this.

Personally, I'm fine with people talking about me behind my back; I just don't want to hear about it. Please don't tell me! I'm a sensitive person, and it's hard for me not to think about that mean comment forever. Everyone will always have their judgments about you, your work, and your choices. Don't even try to manage it. Digital strategist and art authority Kimberly Drew states it perfectly: "I've rarely been to a dinner party or to an event where someone wasn't trying to figure out why I was there. Sometimes you have to trust that you should be there and that's it. You're the one doing the work. Only you know your flaws."

### Ruth Ann Harnisch: Other People's Opinions Are None of Your Business

*"Recovering journalist" turned philanthropist, investor, and "punk rock fairy godmother of feminism," Ruth Ann Harnisch understands that other people will have their own opinions about you.*

"When I was a television newscaster, part of the work included responding to the public's opinion of me—looks, brains, professionalism, clothes, hairstyle, attitude. There were focus groups designed to tell the management how their on-air talent was being perceived. These were brutal. I learned (after sobbing a few times about how ugly and fat they thought I was) this truth: *What you think of me is none of my business*. Most people don't know me, and they have a made-up idea of me if they think of me at all. It's totally their own invention, and it has nothing to do with me. The people who thought I was ugly and fat on television were always shocked to discover that I was petite and kinda cute in real life. This is universally true: Most people don't know you and are making up their version of you through their own lens. It's what you know to be true about yourself that matters, period."

## NEGATIVE CONSEQUENCES

I've been told I'm "too much" (a unique critique that mysteriously seems to be reserved for women—in other words, it's sexist) or too loud. Over time taking this criticism has gotten easier, but the challenge never goes away 100 percent. We are all humans who want to be liked. I could spend time worrying about what other people think, but there will always be others with judgments and comments, and it's not productive.

Chances are I've already said those mean things to myself one million times in my life while applying mascara or eating a sandwich. I don't need a new voice saying it—or new material. We are meanest to ourselves and we are our own worst critics. Silencing that voice inside your head is often harder than silencing a troll. Telling your own personal boogey monster to bug off is some of the hardest work of all.

## Ready, Set, Go!

- **Determine your own personal Nightmare Question.**
- **Answer it.**
- **Practice redirecting conversations to discuss your points and goals. Don't feel stuck answering a question that you don't want to answer—prepare what you will say ahead of time so you can move on.**

# 13

# How to Deal with Being "Out There"

You're never going to be able to please everyone with your voice and message. Period. Don't even begin to try. Sometimes, even getting positive recognition and figuring out how to feel good about it is trickier than dealing with hate. The hate is expected, the positivity is unexpected. We know how to brace ourselves for nasty comments. We're not trained to accept compliments or praise, which is part of Bragging Better—asking for recognition and then appreciating and accepting the attention we deserve. Not only are your accomplishments worth talking about, but the benefits you reap from bragging need to be celebrated and considered.

### Liz Plank: A No Is a Door to Yes

*Liz Plank, television commentator, speaker, award-winning journalist, and author of* For the Love of Men: A New Vision for Mindful Masculinity, *knows a thing or two about fighting for her ideas in a sea of doubt.*

"I had to learn that a no is a door to a yes. Just because someone doesn't like what you have to say, just because someone says you should be saying it differently, it doesn't mean that what you're doing is wrong, and it doesn't mean that you are wrong. I'm still learning to differentiate how I feel about myself, and how I feel about my work, with how other people perceive it, or how other people interpret it.

"When people dare me to shut up, it makes me even more excited about being loud. When people tell me something can't be done, I take it as a dare. I try to take it as a challenge rather than an obstacle."

It's okay to piss people off, too. Anger is a scary emotion to incite, especially for women. Taking a stand and sharing your position proudly with the work to back it up is part of being strong and determined. Your opinions or message aren't going to be pleasing to everyone. Don't mute your passion, even if it's controversial. You need to be prepared for blowback, but if you're primed and ready, making people mad is often a gateway to change.

## Others' Fears and Insecurities Come Out

Let me tell you what's really happening here. Bragging Better and being in public likely illuminates other people's deep-seated insecurities. It has nothing to do with you, but it will make them uneasy. For all of the work you've done to be loud, there are others who wish they had that strength. Instead of being able to say they're jealous, they find it way easier to insult you, call you a name, or say something nasty. That's what their comments really mean. When we see someone doing something we ourselves cannot, we often feel resentful and jealous.

I sat at dinner recently with a woman who told me she initially couldn't stand me. I thought, "I better shove this entire dinner roll into my mouth right now to soften this blow." She said she was annoyed by me when she came to a Women Write Washington (a book series I host in DC for women writers) event and she saw how proud I was of the event, the panel, and the turnout. She even hated how confidently I spoke. We were then seated next to each other at this dinner, and she waited until a few hours in to tell me this because she decided she had changed her mind. This was a brave thing to do, to admit that, because she herself thought she could never do something like that, she told me. And that after hearing my message and speaking to me, she realized that I had set an example for her that made her think she could. It was simultaneously revealing, touching, insulting, and great.

Criticism is important and so is staying grounded in what you know to be true. Pat Mitchell had to learn this the hard way. "It was particularly hard for me at PBS because the criticism comes from every direction: the right, the left, the government, the producers, the stations," said Mitchell. "You're balancing so many needs and all of them diverse. It just was a part of leadership in that case. You have to hold on to what you know is right."

It doesn't mean it's not hard, though. And it doesn't mean you won't slip up and accidentally look at your podcast comments where many people say it's hard to take you seriously because of how your voice sounds! (Can you tell I did that, just now, and it hurt my heart center but also meant that my audience was growing?)

There are ways to respond when someone levels criticism of bragging or being "too much" at you. First, consider the basis of the criticism. It often means one of a few things:

- This person is unable to do the bragging or work that you have done, so you make them uneasy.
- They haven't seen this kind of behavior before. And with something new, instead of accepting it, they are rejecting and criticizing it.
- They tried to do the same, and it didn't work for them. They feel intimidated or threatened, so they would rather shut you down than try again.

Exactly none of these things have anything to do with you. They are all about the other person, who hopes that by criticizing you, you will take on their own anxiety. It still sucks, but it's true.

There's a difference between constructive criticism and just straight-up obnoxious comments. It is important to be able to tell someone who is important to you (not a random internet troll) that their comments are hurtful, even if you feel that they are genuinely trying to help you. People are going to say a lot of things to you when you get out there and they may even feel that they mean well. You might hear it from people very close to you, which is the hardest kind of criticism. I remember someone close to me saying *Brag Better* was just a "bad idea," and I wanted to crawl into a hole and die. Guess it's a book now, sucka!

In my experience the meanest comments can come from other women. While this is a generalization, I believe that women deliver more pointed criticism, layered with nuance and an understanding of each others' experiences.

## Don't Feed the Trolls

What about negative, nasty, anonymous commenters: trolls? For the most part, you should ignore them. Actually, ignoring them—that is, not letting their crap permeate your feelings—is the extra hard work. I still fall prey to the trolls, too, even after ten years of experience.

My best advice is to not engage with the trolls. Do not respond to that post and do not reply to that email. By feeding the trolls and responding to their comments, you're only giving that person attention he doesn't deserve and making it seem like their comments are valid enough to deserve a response. You can set up an email filter to immediately send any keywords to the trash, and you can always mute and block people. There is nothing wrong with shutting someone down and letting that be the message you send. Sometimes the strongest response is no response.

## Just Because You're in Public Doesn't Mean You Owe People Something

When someone is well-known, we have this odd idea that we are close to that person. Whether it's a podcast host you're obsessed with or a superstar like Mariah Carey, we have seen or heard a lot from these people and think we know them. The truth is that we don't. Just because I have consumed every piece of content Jenna Marbles has released for the past decade doesn't mean I truly know her. I know a version of her, but only the version she presents for public consumption.

When we spend time with public people it can make us feel, sometimes, like they owe us something. I remember meeting Natalie Portman, a hero of mine, and asking her for a picture. She said no, and it made me strongly dislike her for years. Many years later I realized that she didn't owe me anything.

Just because you're in public doesn't mean you now have to listen to everyone's two cents or that you owe them your time or attention. Sometimes we think that public figures are there for us, that we should be able to tell our secrets to them or give them feedback about what we think they could do better—and that they are required to listen. That by choosing to be in public they owe us their time and energy, that we own them. That is not true. If someone makes you feel this way, redirect their comments and continue on. Be short, courteous, and just keep moving.

If you're confronted in public with comments or out-of-line questions, Luvvie Ajayi suggests saying something like, "Hey, man, that's not an appropriate question," "I'm not really open to receiving that feedback," or "It's something I don't talk about publicly." You can also ignore the comments completely. Famous people are trained to say things like, "Hey, no photos, no autographs, and I don't do hugs." Instead, they might offer a handshake or a high five, or tell the person that they appreciate them coming up to say hello. You could also simply say, "I keep my private life private, but thank you for enjoying my work."

## How and When to Take Criticism Seriously

"I care a lot about what the people I love think about me," admits Jia Tolentino, *New Yorker* writer and author of *Trick Mirror*, but she makes it clear that she only extends that sentiment to a small circle. "I want to be held accountable and for my behavior to be good, but I want that to be for the people that I know: my friends, my colleagues, my family." Those are the opinions that matter to her, the feedback she chooses to listen to—the rest is, at best, just chatter and, at worst, destructive. "I feel like the internet has the ability to make us feel beholden to strangers, and I tend to think that that's kind of an unhealthy way of living." I couldn't agree more.

Feedback and opinions do matter when they come from a source that will help you grow or that you genuinely care about. You have to be centered in who you are and who you will listen to—those you trust who keep you honest, but also care about you. I know which friends of mine will give me straight-talk advice. I know which friends will simply be supportive no matter what. I also know when to ask for help and guidance. Knowing a range of opinions and having a strong center and people around you will help you eschew comments that aren't helpful. This will require some trial and error. I have a habit of asking one friend for pure validation when she is really a nuts-and-bolts person. I want her to tell me everything is okay, not what to do. But that's my own fault, because that's who she is.

There is professional feedback and criticism beyond your friends, however, that does matter. When evaluating external feedback, first consider the source. Does this person have experience that you do not and that you want?

Thus, should you consider their viewpoint? If so, take it, thank them, and work on it. Just because someone is senior to you doesn't mean you have to take their criticism. You have to decide if the criticism applies to your career, and then decide how to implement it into your own life.

Take criticism seriously when . . .

- It comes from multiple sources you trust.
- It comes from someone you deeply respect and admire.
- It comes from someone whose career path you aspire to follow.
- It comes in a constructive, thoughtful package.

Ignore criticism when . . .

- It comes from the peanut gallery, not people you care about.
- You can tell it is rooted in feelings that aren't good for you or aren't coming from a good place.
- You're told you should ignore it from people you trust.

## Perfect Is Boring

Nobody wants to see a robot all the time, and nobody wants to see perfect 24/7. It's easy to want to slip into that, however, to protect yourself. The Bragging Better strategy includes planning to protect yourself in the public eye.

You don't have to be the perfect person to Brag Better. Part of being out there is putting your authentic self in public. With calculated vulnerability, you can reach more people than you ever thought possible. Understanding which parts of yourself to show takes time and consideration. You don't have to be positive all the time—that isn't real life. Showing your moments of weakness, at least for me, has often garnered the greatest amount of support. Whether that's among friends or a professional group, showing your challenging emotions doesn't make you weak, it actually makes you strong.

Perfect is also boring because you're not having a productive conversation when everyone agrees with you. Perfection is not a badge of honor. In fact, it might mean you're doing something wrong. I think a lot about a particular Instagram influencer who I used to love. She talked about art and culture and had strong opinions. The bigger she got, however, the less she talked about her opinions and deferred to middle-of-the-road, safe content. Her growth has stalled, and I stopped following her. She was trying to stay neutral and please everyone, but more than anything it just made me feel disconnected from her.

You will make mistakes along your bragging journey, and that's a crucial part of learning. You can expect to . . .

- Engage with a troll or someone who doesn't make you feel good and regret it.
- Brag in the wrong place and have it not go well.
- Take criticism seriously even though it comes from an untrustworthy source.

## Bragging Mishaps

Sometimes *bragging worse* happens. This means that either you've misjudged your audience, you've spoken out of turn, or you've used the wrong words. It sucks, but take the time to learn from those mistakes. To be clear, I have made every single one of them myself.

## BRAGGING OVER OTHERS

Sometimes you misjudge the room, as I did in that big speech where I came off like a competitive, obnoxious know-it-all. Make sure you Brag Better not at the expense of others. This practice is often trial and error. You might falter a few times, step on some toes, or look not so great. These experiences will help you understand the right place and time.

## BRAGGING TO THE WRONG AUDIENCE

Sometimes it's not the time and place to brag. Maybe you're in an all-hands meeting where the focus is not on personal wins but the wins of the team. Maybe you didn't read the room and couldn't tell that celebrating wasn't what was on the schedule, that it was more of a conversation about strategy.

## BRAGGING WITH THE WRONG WORDS

Know your audience, but also know the language they're speaking. Going in hard with your self-stats isn't the best way of bragging. Pick up on the language that others are using and make sure to temper your own.

When you screw up, that's okay. You're allowed to grow and learn. If the situation warrants it, apologize. Usually you'll be able to tell from feedback or looks on faces that the brag fell flat and short. When this has happened to me, I sit with what I've done, make the necessary amends, and promise to learn from the experience.

## Let's Celebrate

It's not all gloom and doom. Setting expectations is important, but so is being proud of your work. Bragging Better can be awesome, once you decide to let it. You've done all the work of getting out there and Bragging Better, next is learning how to accept the praise and positive reinforcement. Maybe even flaunt it.

A few ideas to get your party engine going:

- Invite your friends over for a fun activity, dinner, or drinks. I once threw myself a "book deal" party and bought a cake that my friends and I ate on my roof. I sprung for a fancy trendy cake, and it was delicious. I licked the box it came in.
- Email a group of family and close friends with your win, telling them you're proud of it (save the responses you get so you can look back at them and smile).
- Treat yourself to something you wouldn't normally do, like a massage or an indulgent midday movie if you can squeeze it in. My favorite thing to do when I have a super big win is walk into a mid-afternoon movie and turn off my phone. If you can do it, it's calming and pretty liberating.
- Go with your colleagues to happy hour to celebrate your win. Your wins aren't always yours alone, so it's fun to celebrate with those you work with, too. I once scored a big project with a friend who also had her own company, and we made sure to acknowledge it with some margaritas.

It's hard work to make your voice heard, so when you do, you should be proud of your work. That's part of Bragging Better, too—doing the work of bragging, but also giving yourself a big pat on the back for doing it well. As I've said, these practices are not often seen as worthy of time or recognition. Take a minute to realize how far you've come.

### Kimberly Drew: Get in the Habit of Celebrating Yourself

*Kimberly Drew is a social media strategist, art historian, and art critic who makes celebrating herself a habit.*

"I have this thing that I call 'soft goals.' They're little promises that I make to myself about self-improvement, and when I accomplish them, I pause and meditate on the success of this moment. Some things are really nice to just hold to your chest and celebrate the fuck out of. It can be the littlest thing. It's getting in the habit of celebrating yourself. I want people to understand what we have accomplished and be proud of that."

Celebrating your newfound or continuing bragging journey is a practice that will evolve as time goes on. The irony is that you also have to spend time bragging to yourself, sometimes more than others. Our constant desire for improvement makes us good at our jobs, but it can also hinder us from feeling the joy of what we've accomplished.

## ACCEPTING PRAISE AND COMPLIMENTS

I will never forget the comedian Amy Schumer's sketch on her show *Inside Amy Schumer* about a group of female friends complimenting one another. The group goes around saying nice things to each person, while said recipient responds by immediately trashing herself. When it gets to Amy, she decides to accept the compliment and her friends' heads blow off. They are shocked. This is an extreme, funny, and true depiction: Accepting praise and compliments is hard. This is particularly true for women, or any of us who have been taught to overdo the modesty. Or in other words, to not Brag Better.

It's totally possible for you to accept praise without your head blowing off (at a sheer minimum). Acknowledging and accepting someone's compliment, especially when you might not feel that way about yourself, can feel hard and crummy. In the same way that we aren't socialized to Brag Better, we aren't taught to feel that good or nice things merit attention, particularly as women. That's a major bummer. I think you've gotten far enough along in this book to know my thoughts on standing "in the sun" (in the words of Shonda Rhimes) and accepting praise, but that doesn't mean it's not hard, even for me.

When I collaborated on my first book, I was unable to accept praise from others or really from myself. Writing a book is one of the few things I've always known I wanted to do. For a writer, the physical manifestation of your hard work, in a bound book on a shelf, is the ultimate goal. I was successfully working toward my goal. But instead of celebrating, I was head down, furiously writing, obsessively keeping timetables of deadlines and worrying.

Whenever anyone complimented me on the book, I brushed it off instead of accepting the comments. I didn't know how to handle the praise. I shut it down or deflected it. How could I do that and not practice what I preached? I had done something significant and massive for myself, but

I was deflecting all of the comments that came from it. I couldn't accept the good things that came with getting something I wanted.

I deflected the comments because I felt that I didn't deserve them. I had my own internal work to do. Feeling like our accomplishments are worthy is something that is a continued practice. Clearly, I needed to take my own advice. I also wasn't making space for a huge part of Bragging Better—accepting the praise you worked so hard to get. What was the point of doing all of the work for the recognition, just to shoot it down? I heard myself doing it, and eventually I was able to make myself stop. But I did some damage first. I think back to scenarios when people wanted to celebrate me for a giant accomplishment, and I didn't let them. I'm sure it was not only confusing, but it stopped them from potentially offering me other stepping-stones in my career.

Letting others celebrate your accomplishments can make you feel good, let your legacy carry on, and also bring goodwill and joy to those around you.

When you Brag Better, allow yourself to feel good feelings and reap the benefits of your hard work. It's so important to recognize this along the way. We spend a lot of time reaching for the things we want and doing things that might not be comfortable. It takes time and skill to pause and experience the good feels right before you move on to the next thing. The first time you choose to brag—in whatever form it takes—is a win. Write it down. Make a list of your brags that you can celebrate.

## Ready, Set, Go!

- Keep a running document of your brags, both big and small.
- Each time you reach a bragging milestone, stop and do something that makes you feel good. (Maybe it's the same thing each time. Is it a dance, a special dessert, or something else that you love?)
- With a big win, email those close to you and ask them to help you celebrate.
- Have a bragging buddy—someone who knows how hard this is for you and who can remind you each time you do it well.
- Practice accepting a compliment from someone.

# 14

# How to Help Others Brag Better

Because someone else Bragged Better for me, this book was able to see the light of day. It showed me the power of being in the right place at the right time, but also the incredible privilege of being on the receiving end of someone's brags.

I had been crafting this book on and off since 2013. I had "brag" down, and I knew I wanted it to be a book that showed the power of hyping yourself. I had pushed and pulled, getting everyone to listen to the concept, but breaking through was hard.

Then I gave a speech to one of my favorite audiences, the UN Foundation's Girl Up Leadership Summit. This gathering hosts incredible young women from around the country and world for topics on everything from empowerment to education. Kate Schatz, the best-selling author of multiple books on women in history, decided to sit in on my "Brag Better" talk after she herself was done speaking. I remember seeing her in the audience, but since I hadn't met her yet, I assumed she was someone's mom or a conference organizer, since the rest of the crowd was made up of high schoolers and college-aged women. It turned out to be an incredible, lucky duck moment. I was in the right place at the right time, but Kate decided to Brag Better on my behalf.

After the talk, Kate approached me to ask if I had considered making "Brag Better" into a book. Had I ever. She convinced me to send my materials to her, which I was afraid to do because I had dealt with a bunch of rejection on the topic. I spoke to my best friend about it, who pushed me to do it and told me I had nothing to lose (another example of someone else Bragging Better on my behalf). So I sent a draft of *Brag Better* to Kate, and then Kate offered to vouch for me and to make a big connection to her editor. She had absolutely no reason to do so, other than being a good person who wanted to help spread my strong message. Kate's editor, in turn, introduced me to my agent who helped bring this book into the open today and into your very hands or ears at this current moment. I am a true beneficiary of someone who decided to Brag Better for a message she believed in. I will never forget this act of kindness. I am grateful and determined to pay it forward.

Bragging Better isn't just about you.

In fact, Bragging Better has just as much to do with how you help others rise, too. Not only is it impossible to win alone, but also you need others to spread your message. Just as important is reaching out to share and elevate the voices around you. A core tenet of this book is how to boost your voice, but also how to boost others' voices so we all win.

It's easier for The Qualified Quiet to brag about someone else, so acting on behalf of another person will allow you to lean in to a skill set you might already have. According to a survey called "The Self-Promotion Gap," several women-owned companies found that 80 percent of men and 84 percent of women reported feeling somewhat or very comfortable talking about other people's accomplishments. The survey found that the only way people could have that same level of comfort talking about their own accomplishments was if they were talking to friends and family. Only about 40 percent of people felt comfortable discussing their own accomplishments with strangers, on social media, or in front of a crowd. It's so much easier to tout someone else.

## There's Plenty of Space on the Stage

Part of Bragging Better is realizing that there is enough space for the recognition of everyone. You are not in competition with everyone else—you are in competition with yourself to bring the best, most authentic you to your work every day. We've perpetuated a myth that there are only a certain number of slots that we, particularly as women, are competing for. This is not true. There are enough press outlets, conferences, promotions, and projects for everyone. If a conference is booked, you can pitch them for next year. If there is a project you wanted but didn't get, a new opportunity will pop up.

### JEALOUSY IS POINTLESS

Jealousy is an enemy of Bragging Better, but it's been my personal Achilles' heel forever. Jealousy holds you back from cultivating your own ideas, being proud of your own accomplishments, and thinking freely and openly. We give up too much of our brains real estate to jealousy, and all of that space could be used for healthier thoughts. I've seen the practice of jealousy hurt people's careers, too. They spend so much time being jealous that they are unable to see what great things they have going on. This is incredibly easy to do in our current era, one of shiny, beautiful Instagram posts and perfect veneers.

We put a literal filter on our lives to make them look more attractive. It's important to talk openly about the less "beautiful" parts of our lives. Life is messy, and it's not all beauty. That's what makes it interesting. Envy is a really tough emotion to deal with, and we all deal with it no matter where we are in our careers and lives. A *Harvard Business Review* roundup found that "regardless of the economic climate, people at all levels of a firm are vulnerable to envy. However, it intensifies in times of economic crisis. As losses mount, employees worry that they're in jeopardy and grow to resent successful colleagues."

It's scary and hard to be a professional today, particularly in an economy that is shifting toward freelancing, with difficult, expensive healthcare and an extremely high cost of living. It makes jealousy that much easier to slip into. A longitudinal study of eighteen thousand adults in Australia found some interesting results about envy: "The young are especially susceptible [to envy]. Levels of envy fall as people grow older." The same study found there is "no evidence . . . that envy acts as a useful motivator. Greater envy is associated with slower—not higher—growth of psychological well-being in the future. Nor is envy a predictor of later economic success."

This means jealousy can only hurt you. It's hard to look at these statistics and not think about how you can make jealousy a smaller part of your life.

## SHINE THEORY

Instead of feeding those feelings of doubt toward yourself and negativity toward others, put them aside, with some time and practice and boundaries. When you Brag Better, those around you do, too. Your actions inspire people to look inside themselves for what their special message is so that they, too, can be proud, loud, and strategic about it. You are leading by example, not by leaving people in the dust.

The idea that a rising tide lifts all boats is something that has been continuously refined and amplified thanks to podcast cohosts, authors of the book *Big Friendship*, businesswomen, and best friends Aminatou Sow and Ann Friedman. They have spent years developing Shine Theory. While much has been discussed on the power of hyping your friends in *Brag Better*, Sow and Friedman have nailed Shine Theory down into detailed canon.

According to Sow and Friedman:

> Shine Theory is an investment, over the long term, in helping someone be their best self—and relying on their help in return. It is a conscious decision to bring your full self to your friendships, and to not let insecurity or envy ravage them. Shine Theory is a commitment to asking, "Would we be better as collaborators than as competitors?" The answer is almost always yes.

People know you by the company you keep. Shine Theory is recognizing that true confidence is infectious, and if someone is tearing you down or targeting you as competition, it's often because they are lacking in confidence or support themselves. It's a practice of cultivating a spirit of genuine happiness and excitement when your friends are doing well, and being there for them when they aren't.

My best friend is my biggest champion and I am hers, which exemplifies Shine Theory. She has a job that is more behind-the-scenes than mine, and she's always showing up to watch me speak despite working long hours. She was on a panel not too long ago, and it was a big deal. She doesn't do much public-facing work, but you can bet that I showed up nearly with my face painted for a football game. I stopped short of a foam finger. I made sure to get there early and sit in the front row. I took lots of pictures and playfully embarrassed her with her name placard. I made her pose next to the podium. I was so happy that she was doing well and that I was there to celebrate her. Then, of course, I made her brag about it.

Friedman and Sow walk their talk and put their principles into practice, both as a pair and as sole creators. "We both truly love and respect each other's work, experience, and perspective. So, we are legitimately excited to be linked together as collaborators. That said, we are definitely individuals and we both have different qualities and skills we want to be known for. We try to check in with each other, openly and regularly, about how our collaborative work fits in to each of our overall career pictures, because we will always each have our own thing going on." Each woman recognizes the value in the other's individual voice and works to uplift it—even when they're sharing the proverbial stage. "On the podcast, our voices are separate. We are in dialogue with each other, and while we often agree, part of the value in the show is that we each bring different perspectives to the conversation. So, we don't want them to blend!" It's a balance they work to maintain through ample communication and keeping their friendship at the forefront.

Shine Theory goes beyond your close friends, too. A woman in my extended network regularly attends my events and shows up for me. While we aren't super close, I have been struck by her willingness to support my work. She was putting on an event with a big tech brand, and although she didn't say it, I could tell it was a big deal for her. I signed up to attend and she was shocked and delighted when I walked in, and since I knew some of the organizers, I was happy to help her look good to the powers that be. I talked her up to the people that had hired her and helped her strategize on how to promote the work she had spoken about that night. I know it meant a lot to her, but it also felt like it was my duty to help her shine, too.

Allowing us all to shine together is also about building a strong tribe around you. Management executive Cleo Kim focuses on her ability to weather professional storms by cultivating a strong network of like-minded individuals and those who will always hold her up. "It goes back to that tribe that you build around you," says Kim. "That diverse network of people, advisors, caregivers, caretakers, those that you love, because they uplift you when you fall, and they'll be there with you to also navigate risky opportunities." You don't have to bear it all alone. Nobody gets far by trying to do it all themselves. "I know that cultivating that tribe around me is going to be really important when unexpected headwinds come, and so I don't feel alone and need to bear it by myself," Kim says.

## Keah Brown: Seek Out People Whose Lived Experiences Exist Outside of Your Own

*Keah Brown is a writer and disability activist. She is the creator of #DisabledAndCute and the author of the book* The Pretty One: On Life, Pop Culture, Disability, and Other Reasons to Fall in Love with Me.

"Finding inclusive voices takes time. You have to really be in a place to actively do the inclusive work and not have to worry about apologizing later. For me, it's definitely about effort and opportunities, making sure that we seek people outside of our friend groups and our lived experiences. . . . Seek out people whose lived experiences exist outside of your own."

A 2014 study of white-collar workers in Norway found that "greater female representation at higher ranks narrows the gender gap in promotion rates at lower ranks." In other words, women higher up the food chain were helping women further down.

When you help someone gain visibility, it does not reduce yours. When you gain traction, it helps those around you instead of hurting them. Plus, having work friends is good for you. The polling firm Gallup reports that having a friend at work is highly related to job satisfaction and productivity, particularly for women. "Our research has repeatedly shown a concrete link between having a best friend at work and the amount of effort employees expend in their job. For example, women who strongly agree they have a best friend at work are more than twice as likely to be engaged (63 percent) compared with the women who say otherwise (29 percent)." Gallup also found that companies where more employees were friends with one another reported fewer safety incidents, higher profits, and more engaged customers.

## The Brag Breakdown with Kimberly Drew: Use Your Voice to Shine a Light for Others

*Discovering the power of Black artists transformed the work and career of Kimberly Drew, creator of the popular Tumblr blog* Black Contemporary Art. *She has used her growing platforms to show the art world the importance of Black artists, and she is conscious of her ability to help others shine.*

### Learn First

"I had this aha moment learning about Black artists, learning names that I've never heard before, and I immediately was just like, 'Okay, I have to do something with this,' and [learning has] been my ethos as a person since. . . . I learned the names of five Black artists, which became five thousand Black artists, and became this entire career."

### Choose Optimism

"Fear is what can get us to that point where [we think], 'There's no room for me. No one who looks like me,' and [we haven't] even [achieved our goal] yet. So how can we be more imaginative about the possibilities of this field? I swear to you, optimism is the only thing we have. If I had gone through this same exact career and life with pessimism, I assure you, I would not have made it this far. . . . Don't fill in every blank with doom because [that's] not doing yourself any favors."

### Fear Yourself, Not Institutions

"I'm more afraid of myself than I am of any institution. Letting [myself] down, I just can't do it. . . . I'm not going to be ashamed of myself. I'm not going to put myself in a situation where I'm like, 'I should have said that.' There are definitely moments when I do go home and think, 'Yup, you really didn't speak up today,' and all I can think about are the ten things that will happen because I didn't. . . . Speaking up can be hard, but I just know that I don't want to go home disappointed in myself."

## OTHER BENEFITS OF BRAGGING FOR OTHERS

Bragging Better for others can also bring you true joy; I know it does for me.

I was working with a media organization to help them find diverse and interesting voices for an event that was on the West Coast. I thought about the people I knew that were talking about inclusion, fighting for more women and men of color, LGBTQ+ people, and beyond to make sure their voices were heard. I was not a fit for this speaking gig—as a white woman, my experience in diversity was not nearly enough to thoughtfully contribute. So, I worked on paying it forward. I selected two friends I was close with, who both ended up being on the stage for this event, killing it with their thoughts and time, and elevating their own voices and profiles at the same time.

For one friend, this led to a significant new piece of business. Being on this media entity's panel allowed him to showcase his opinions. I was so proud because my friends were getting the recognition they deserved. My other friend added invaluable advice to this media organization—one that was pretty old, white, and male—and even challenged the conference organizers themselves to think bigger and better. What a gift to the conference.

I was able to watch two of my friends, whose work I care about, do well. It made me so happy to be able to pass the mic, promote those I love, and watch them win, too. Part of this is the job of paying it forward when you are someone who people listen to.

Luvvie Ajayi knows the power of paying it forward to encourage the voices of those we haven't heard. "When we have the mic, where we have the power, our job is to disrupt the space. And also to insist that we pass on the mic to somebody who typically would not be handed the mic. The idea that privilege is limitless," she says. Ajayi encourages big corporations to ask interns to come to and participate in meetings. She considers that a large part of her job, to "make sure that other people of power in the world are being challenged to use their power better, to use their power successfully and to tap on their power."

It can also be powerful to consider going the extra mile to make sure you're elevating the voices in every arena of your life, even those you don't know. For Natalia Oberti Noguera—creator and host of *Pitch Makeover,* a podcast on startups, pitching, investing, and #morevoices—that means considering, "Where am I having this breakfast meeting? Is the chef or any of the owners a woman, a nonbinary person, or [a person] of color? And does it take a little bit more extra work to do the research? Yes." But she says it's worth it in the long run. For Oberti Noguera, "inclusion is a daily practice." It's a muscle we can all learn to flex.

### Kimberly Drew: Humility Is the Grandest Thing

*For writer and art authority Kimberly Drew, being humble is essential.*

"The playing field that I'm working on is 'Excellence is the bare minimum,' which is just what it means to be a professional Black woman. Sometimes excellence is our only option.

"Some people [ask me], 'I'm white. What can I do?' The first thing you can do is understand that maybe you can't do anything. I think that moving through spaces with humility is always really helpful . . . [and] the assumption that you have more power because of your privilege is bullshit. . . . Humility is the grandest thing."

## IT FEELS REALLY GOOD TO RECEIVE

I've also had visible people who didn't need to promote me do so, and it has made a tremendous difference in my life. Whether it's visible women in business networks or someone I admire, it has been amazing to have my work shared. One distinct moment was when Shonda Rhimes (yes, the television producer Shonda Rhimes) tweeted an article I wrote. When I first saw it, I was convinced it was fake. A friend had screenshotted it and sent it to me. I immediately pulled up Rhimes's Twitter feed, and there it was. Holy crap. I yelped, in what was then my tiny broom closet of an office. I stopped what I was doing, did a little shimmy, and then told everyone I knew about it. It feels so good to be on the receiving end of someone's brags about you. Celebrate that and create it for those around you.

Celebrating the accomplishments of those you are close to can make your relationships even closer. By celebrating those around you in your community and beyond, you are being a good citizen.

## How to Brag about Your Colleagues and Contemporaries

A 2014 study found that "an emotional culture of companionate love at work positively relates to employees' satisfaction and teamwork and negatively relates to their absenteeism and emotional exhaustion."

When it comes to your coworkers and colleagues, asking them how you can help their hype means a lot but also makes sure you aren't in a situation where they aren't on the same page as you.

### WHAT DOES YOUR COLLEAGUE NEED?

There are many ways that you can brag about and promote your colleagues. The first is to simply ask what she needs. As I've said, everyone is on a different Brag Better path, and some want to be more front and center than others. The first step is asking your colleagues what you can do to promote their work, make them feel heard, and help them win.

You'd be surprised what people want when they are asked, and you are displaying one of the important pillars of Bragging Better, which is to pass the microphone and work to be an advocate. Sometimes people just want to feel heard without a direct action. This means taking the time not to amplify their brags, but to sit with their comments and tell people that they matter. Sometimes it's also just a matter of knowing someone else cares enough to ask in the first place. It can be smaller acknowledgments versus big brags that are helpful, too.

## SUPPORTING YOUR COLLEAGUES IN A MEETING

Then there are other tactical ways to help boost those around you at work. In meetings, echoing the sentiments of colleagues whose work you like cosigns their ideas and makes them appear more powerful to the decision makers. The actual repeating of someone else's words and ideas makes those words more impactful. Science backs this up. On the negative side, back in 1977 researchers found that by repeating false statements over and over subjects were more likely to rate them as true. However, you can use this principle in the service of good. Your colleagues' truthful accomplishments will seem more valid if people hear about them multiple times from multiple sources.

You can also serve as someone's strategic ally in meetings. By teaming up with a colleague you can raise both of your voices together. I've gone into many meetings with collaborators where we've teed up good questions for one another. I've prepared leading statements that I know will make the other person look good. Take the time before a big meeting or presentation to find a buddy to Brag Better with.

You can also make it clear to your colleagues' bosses that you think they are valuable. This requires consent and consideration, but when it comes to raises, annual reviews, or other benchmarks, the praise of others moves the needle. Ask a colleague if you can talk him or her up to the person in charge. When you talk to the boss, show her how someone on her team is of value.

I did this once for a big client project. I wanted to hire a specific partner, someone I knew was smart, really on her game, and would be a perfect fit. But first I had to convince my client, who wouldn't immediately understand the value of the partner I wanted to hire. So, I did a little strategizing with the potential partner first. And a little matchmaking on both ends. I uncovered their common interest outside of work and talked to each of them about it. I sung their praises to each other. And then I showed my cards a little and gave the woman I wanted to hire some inside information. I told her how to frame her argument, showcase her work, and what amount to quote knowing how the client wanted to see information. It worked like a charm. She was speaking his language. They talked about movies for two hours, he was late to his next meeting, and she landed the gig. It's fun to play professional matchmaker, to see everyone win, and in this case, produce a much superior work product.

## HELPING THOSE MORE JUNIOR TO YOU

This isn't just a strategy for your contemporaries, but also for those above and below you.

Those junior to you will be looking to you not only to set an example but also to reach back and help those coming up behind you. This is yet another part of the Bragging Better ethos.

I'll never forget when a very senior entrepreneur vouched for me with a prominent publication. I didn't think I had any shot at working with them, and there was no reason she needed to help promote me other than that she believed in me and wanted me to succeed. This boosted my confidence and gave me the strength to submit my pitches, which the publication accepted and published. Without her endorsement and also her nudge, a lot of my initial writing wouldn't have seen the light of day.

Giving credit to your colleagues, both junior and senior, also helps them do the same for you, feel confident, and continue the practice with others. In the way that the senior entrepreneur helped me, I have a responsibility to do the same. Your bragging on someone's behalf can affect someone's entire career trajectory. Share credit, give credit, and if you have a win and someone junior helped you on the project, shout him or her out, too. If your boss is looking to promote someone or assign someone to a new important project, recommend a colleague or subordinate you think is worthy of the job.

## BETTER TOGETHER

I trained someone who had trouble speaking up in meetings. I told her to find a buddy and confide in that person that she was shy but knew this participation mattered and she needed help. That help could come in the form of her confidante tossing her a lead-in to a question or just simply agreeing with her audibly. Either action would be tremendously helpful. There is also a lot of research to support these claims. When sentiments are echoed by colleagues, particularly if that initial voice is a woman, it makes people hear those thoughts better.

The Obama White House regularly experienced women doing this for each other.

> When President Obama took office, two-thirds of his top aides were men. Women complained of having to elbow their way into important meetings. And when they got in, their voices were sometimes ignored. So female staffers adopted a meeting strategy they called "amplification": When a woman made a key point,

> other women would repeat it, giving credit to its author. This forced the men in the room to recognize the contribution—and denied them the chance to claim the idea as their own. Obama noticed, [the female aides] said, and began calling more often on women and junior aides.

You can do the same in reverse, too.

There was a piece of business I really wanted, and I wanted to work on it with another business owner friend that I adored. We plotted together, having several meetings about how to approach the business development angle and play off each other's strengths. We wrote out scripts, teeing up questions to the potential client and each other that would make us each shine, looking capable and perfect for the job. We also mapped out some key agreements and disagreements—all were part of a strategy to get the job. Instead of competing, we were stronger together when we amplified each other's voices. It was a fun exercise, and we killed it. We got the contract.

## The Brag Breakdown with Jessica Bennett: Find a Boast Bitch

*For Jessica Bennett, writer for the* New York Times *and author of* Feminist Fight Club, *finding an ally to Brag Better with has been a way to flourish in her career. Bennett has coined this partner-in-brag a "boast bitch" and tells us how to find our own.*

### Why You Need a Boast Bitch

"I call it a 'boast bitch.' This person boasts for you. You boast for them. The research shows that by boasting on behalf of someone else, you look really selfless and good and like you're a good colleague and teammate. And simultaneously, the person for whom you are boasting or affirming gets credit for their work.

"I was pretty honest about some of the struggles that I faced, and being nervous about pitching ideas in meetings, or feeling like they weren't heard, or griping about how my ideas would get attributed to someone else. [My boast bitch was] a friend who was also an ally."

### Listen and Pay Attention

"There are a couple of studies that have looked at that concept of a person giving an idea and how people in the room in a mixed-gender setting remember that idea in the future, and they are likely to remember it as having come from the man. . . . If you're not attuned to it, or if you don't know that these are institutional issues, you might not notice. Who's being interrupted more? Who's taking up the airspace? Did my boss remember that idea as having come from the wrong person? If it isn't me, can I correct that to make sure they know that it came from someone else?"

### My Boast Dude

"I had a male colleague when I was a junior reporter at *Newsweek*. We had this agreement: During pitch meetings, we would nod vigorously when the other one pitched ideas. The idea was to show to the rest of the room that it was a good thought. I, in particular, felt like I had trouble being heard. He happened to be a white man who was very well respected. . . . Did I have to do this? Did I have to have him? No. But did it work? Yes."

**Reciprocate the Boast**

"It's the simplest solution to a pervasive problem. It may not work every single time, but there's no reason not to try it. . . . You don't necessarily need to be like, 'Will you be my boast bitch?' But you can do it on behalf of someone else."

Bragging Better for others brings so much joy into your life. It also helps you pay it forward, and it helps others learn to step into the spotlight. It's not always easy to share, especially at the office, but in the end we all win.

## KNOWING WHEN TO STEP BACK

It is possible to brag too hard for others, and I know because I've put my foot in my mouth and done it. I was so proud of a friend at an event we were both attending. I noticed she was talking to someone in her industry and it looked like it was going well. Instead of leaving her be, I stuck myself into the conversation. I started to brag all about her to this person in her industry, and she gave me a slightly panicked look. I thought she was being bashful, and I didn't read her body language. She was doing everything short of kicking me to get me to stop, but I carried on talking her up, too busy with my own agenda to make her shine.

As it turns out, the person she was talking to had a complex relationship with some of her work; they knew her already, and it was messy. I had inadvertently made the tension worse. I did my friend a disservice. I blew past her signals and didn't listen. I looked like a jerk and certainly felt like one, too.

My Bragging Better is always evolving. I still work toward

better listening around Bragging Better for others. Learning to Brag Better means that we learn to lift our friends and colleagues up, too, but we must also understand what our friends need from us in that moment.

## Brag Begets Brag

One exciting part about Bragging Better is that it will send a message to other members of The Qualified Quiet who need to hear it—that it's cool to be proud of yourself and say so. You are leading by example, showing off, and literally modeling for someone who might not have known that it was okay to consider singing their own praises.

You cannot be what you cannot see. So, it's so crucial that other members of The Qualified Quiet see you Bragging Better so that they can consider taking that path for themselves. Show other members of The QQ that being proud, loud, and strategic is a win and a key strength.

When all of us Brag Better, everyone will advance ideas across the board. Getting more members of The Qualified Quiet to Brag Better means that the ideas we share, the businesses we create, and the national conversations we have will be filled with additional experienced voices. For us to build a better nation and better workplaces, we need all voices to be heard, not just those who are already talking the loudest. We need you.

### MEN HELPING WOMEN

We touched on having others help amplify your voice. However, this is particularly powerful for female voices. There are countless studies that show that we take women's voices less seriously, and it truly has to change.

This is where men come in. The goal here isn't to crowd out the men or get them to shut up. Instead, we want the men in the room to help us Brag Better. To the men reading this book: we really need you, and we cannot do this alone. According to the *Harvard Business Review*: "The evidence shows that when men are deliberately engaged in gender inclusion programs, 96 percent of organizations see progress, compared to only 30 percent of organizations where men are not engaged."

Men's voices are so powerful that sometimes women are forced to make up fake ones. Like the amazing case of Penelope Gazin and Kate Dwyer, the two founders of art marketplace startup Witchsy. They added a fake male cofounder—Keith Mann—to their pitch materials, and it got them better responses from investors. "It was like night and day," Dwyer told *Fast Company*. "It would take me days to get a response, but Keith could not only get a response and a status update, but also be asked if he wanted anything else or if there was anything else that Keith needed help with."

Men tend to have more social capital and elite connections than comparable women. It's totally unfair—hello, old boys' club. In a 2004 study of high-level business and political leaders, "men generally reported wider ranges of personal contacts with other elites in the political, economic and civil society spheres." So, if men really want to be allies, they can use that social capital for good. Use your power for good, please.

Do you have female colleagues whose voices you could echo? Great. Make room for women in meetings and on stages, and think about how you can use your already amplified voice for positive change. Simply reinforcing a colleague's sentiments if you're a man makes them more valid.

We have a long way to go, but that's a small, simple action you can take today. And one that I believe is part of your job. This can be done for a client or on a business email chain. Bolster the voices of those around you. It will also allow you to ask the same in return.

Elevating the voices of women goes beyond simply echoing them. Consider diverse voices for projects big and small. Does this campaign have gender parity? Racial parity? Age parity? It's time to open your eyes.

For example, the male director of the National Institutes of Health pledged to never do an all-male panel again. He wrote: "Too often, women and members of other groups underrepresented in science are conspicuously missing in the marquee speaking slots at scientific meetings and other high-level conferences. Starting now, when I consider speaking invitations, I will expect a level playing field, where scientists of all backgrounds are evaluated fairly for speaking opportunities. If that attention to inclusiveness is not evident in the agenda, I will decline to take part."

We don't need any more all-male or particularly all-white-male panels, or "manels." It's in men's self-interest to avoid all-male panels or lists, because people *will* notice it, and the backlash will diminish the men involved. You're cutting out many voices, but also cutting out a lot of potential business and customers. It's much better to be part of a diverse panel or list. We need voices that reflect what the world looks like, and that's a much more diverse world than the one that's currently on display.

## Pat Mitchell: It Begins with Believing Women's Voices Matter

*The cofounder of TEDWomen knows the value of women's voices.*

"When I say to a man, or to some men, 'I'm going to a women's conference in Beijing,' I can tell by the questions that follow that there's still this perception that women's conferences are a gabfest. There's a dismissiveness to the concept of women coming together. Never mind that in these four days, fifty women leaders came up with a whole new approach to climate justice.

"It begins with believing women's voices matter. They not only matter because that's the right thing; they matter because they're actually putting new ideas into the universe at just the time we need them. . . . It begins with valuing a woman's voice and then encouraging it."

## Ready, Set, Go!

- **Pick a friend to brag about. Do you have a friend or colleague who needs help having her voice and contributions acknowledged? Is there someone at work who rarely gets the chance to speak up? Focus on people whose voices and ideas have been underrepresented and need to be heard.**
- **Ask someone how you can help promote her. Be sure to ask how they want to be supported, and how they don't want to be supported.**
- **Brag about a colleague or work contact. Do it in a way that makes them feel good.**

# 15

# Ask Others to Brag for You, Too

You are responsible for asking others to promote you, and also letting them know when it works for you and when it doesn't. Don't make them guess. You want everyone to be coming from a position of power.

You'll need to know what you want and be able to tell people what you want them to do, because they might or likely won't know on their own. This might make others uncomfortable, or they might want to help in their own way. You must communicate how others can help amplify you, whether it's sharing something you've written, passing a message along to their friends, or simply just congratulating you. Take time to think about what you want out of the visibility, and how others can help you.

Asking for help can be as simple as saying, "Will you help me amplify my new article or speech?" But as we've discussed, everyone is on a different bragging journey. Plus, we're all busy. This means that when you ask others to promote you, you'll have to hand it to them on a silver platter. In other words, you need to make it very easy for them to help you. That might mean you write the "suggested copy" of a tweet or Facebook share or the blurb praising your work on a project. It ensures that the language this person uses will help you. You have to make it easy for others to help you shine.

## Asking for Support

Sometimes asking for someone to Brag Better for you just means asking for support.

Bringing your colleagues and coworkers in to your own personal struggles might feel hard. You want to seem like you have it all under control. You might be doing more damage than you realize by trying to shoulder work that could be done quicker, better, and in a healthier way by reaching out to others.

I'd bet your coworkers want to help you shine, but they don't know how to help until you ask them. Consider asking them for support by saying, "I want to make sure that I show the higher-ups how great my work on this project was. Would you be open to echoing that along with me in a meeting?" You might consider sending an email to an admin of a Listserv you're both a part of and asking, "Hey, I wrote this article. Can you help me get it out to this great group?" You might also ask for a more public share, whether it be a tweet or Instagram, with language formulated for your audience.

Asking others to brag for you doesn't just mean pure visibility, it also means bringing your name up when it matters. For example, I remind clients that if they are happy with my work, I would be very grateful for their referral. I didn't ask directly for referrals at first, because I was afraid it was "too much." It was not, of course; I need more clients, always. Being brave enough to ask led to several new business relationships. You can also ask a colleague to put in a good word with your boss or ask a friend with a larger social media platform to share something you've done.

## A BIG ASK

It's important to ask others to brag for you, but it's also important to understand how many opportunities you have to do so, and when the right time is to ask. Busy, successful people help others shine, but in limited quantities, and they do it with care, poise, and consideration.

Now, who could you ask for an endorsement or help getting ahead? You can often determine who these people are by working backward. Make a list of people you admire, beginning with those in your industry. I admire those who have carved out a unique path and are true to themselves. Pick traits that are important to you; maybe you like how someone has navigated the spotlight or how someone has risen in the ranks, and decide if you would feel comfortable reaching out to that person and asking for their help in promoting your work.

Just because you do reach out to someone you admire doesn't mean that person will necessarily aid your career. You have to test the waters by being courteous and straightforward, but sometimes it's not the people you expect in your industry that end up being the biggest help. For me, a lot of hype has come from incredible people that I least expected to share my work. Sometimes you have to think outside the realm in which you work to gain insight and mentorship. I love having mentors in industries really different from mine, because conversations with them are illuminating. It helps me gain perspective from a different area of expertise.

Start small with these asks. A decade ago, I decided that I wanted to befriend a coworker I admired. She was funny and cool, and seemed like she really knew her stuff. I'm lucky she decided I was okay, but I approached her by asking if she could give me a bit of advice on a highly specific part of my job. She was open to it, and from there I was able to build a relationship. Don't just go straight to the top; it's good to surround yourself with people at any level who make you better and have a range of opinions.

## WHAT ARE YOU ASKING FOR?

The first thing to decide is, What are you asking this person for, specifically? Are you asking this person to share something about you with their networks? If so, that's a big ask and endorsement. Consider carefully when asking for someone to vouch for you publicly. I do have an audience, but sometimes when people ask me to share about them, I don't. I am not always sure that I want to immediately vouch for them and share with a group I consider precious—the people that follow me. You should consider that as well.

But that doesn't mean you shouldn't try. Emma Gray, author of *A Girl's Guide to Joining the Resistance* and *Huffington Post* senior women's reporter, recommends that you reach out "to someone you admire and ask them for a coffee. Take the risk, send a DM, send an email. If you don't hear back, no harm/no foul, but making human connections and just having real conversations with people that have gone down the career path you want before you is a good place to start," says Gray. It doesn't have to be a giant ask or a request to read your material. You can make a simpler request to get to know someone who came before you in a way that honors their experiences and knowledge.

Maybe you just want them to see your brag. I remember doing this with an influential person I admired. I wasn't about to ask them to share it with their network, but I wanted to send it to her because I thought it would be of interest. I sent her an email wishing her well, and I said, "I wanted to send you this article I wrote because I thought it was up your alley." Just having her acknowledge it was a giant win. Your Bragging Better doesn't have to result in an immediate share—some of your efforts are part of a long-term game and the payoff won't be visible right away. Planting that seed is just as crucial. You can always come back to it later.

## DECIDE WHO TO ASK

Now that you've decided to ask someone to promote you, it's important to figure out who your targets are. I keep Excel spreadsheets of dream asks, which is a list of people who, if they promoted my work, would cause me to faint from joy (top of that list: Michelle Obama, duh). Think big, dream big, and don't be afraid to work backward from the top of the top. Is it Oprah?

You want to make asks that reinforce your goals of Bragging Better. Whether your goal is a new job or a TV gig, skew your asks toward people who can help you get to that goal. Make a targeted list and work on collecting each person's contact information. The more famous the person, the more likely you will have to go through someone else to get to them, so cultivate relationships with assistants and managers, too. The person who I chose to share the article with was a name in fashion, an industry I have made clear that I care about. I work in sustainable and resale fashion, and eventually I want to interview her for my podcast. Instead of asking that straight out—because I know she's busy and interviews are tiring and take time—I decided instead to just open that door and make a connection before asking for anything. I was clear about my intention to cultivate a relationship with her, and it's important enough that I'm comfortable taking my time about it.

## HOW TO ASK

Making an ask is the scary part, but taking your shot is important. First, gather the courage. Second, assuming you're going to be making these asks via email, sit down at your computer and take a deep breath. Always draft these big asks without including the person's email address in the draft, in case you accidentally hit "send." There is nothing worse than not having your ask be as strong as possible and accidentally sending it in the middle of a sentence. Keep it short, like we discussed with a pitch: actionable, direct, and with context, and tell that person what you would like from him or her as explicitly as possible. Be polite, always.

Here are a few big asks with language that has worked for me in the past.

Asking visible people to share my work:

> Hello! I loved your (article, tweet, something that you looked up that the person has done recently). I'm reaching out to share an article I wrote. I'd be so honored if you took a read, and really grateful if you would share it. Here is the link: (insert link). Here is a tweet I crafted if you want to share it: "I loved

> Meredith's article on fly-fishing so much, read it here: (insert link)."

Asking for a testimonial or reference:

> (Name), it was so great to work with you. I really loved how you (compliment them here about their work style or a choice they made during the project). I'm reaching out to ask if you'd be open to writing a testimonial for the FinePoint website. Previous endorsements from past clients have helped my business immensely. Thank you for the consideration.

## WHEN TO ASK

Save a big ask for when you really need it. Find the time that works for you and for them. I'll give you an example. I wanted an endorsement to win a project that would be huge for me. There was someone in my Rolodex that I knew I was allowed exactly one ask like this because he gets asked for things from people all the time. He is very important, busy, and runs a household-name company. So, I had to get strategic and understand that I did in fact want the "when" to be now. I then had to consider the "when" for him—what day of the week should I email him? What time of day? Did I need to find his assistant and loop him or her in?

I was really nervous, and I carefully wrote and reread my email for weeks. I worked up the courage to send it. I was so worried he would say no because my email had language it shouldn't have ("don't worry if this is a no!"). I decided it would be very, very dumb of me not to at least take the swing. I decided the perfect day was Wednesday—not too close to the Monday onslaught of emails and not too close to the weekend. I decided on early afternoon, around 2:00 p.m., so that maybe he would have had a nice lunch and just gotten back to his desk. I made educated guesses based on what I knew about him, how he worked, and what his schedule looked like.

It was a big ask because I was asking him to lend his name to mine, so I considered what that would mean to him and the timing of my asking. He replied immediately with a lovely two-sentence endorsement.

I could easily have gotten a no or a non-answer. Perhaps he was too busy with meetings that week, that month, or even that calendar year (I've experienced all of these scenarios after plucking up the courage to make the ask). Asking is the hard part. Respect someone's boundary if they say they can't be the person to help you at that moment in time. Your graciousness will lead to their respecting you back.

## WHAT NOW?

You spend all this time and energy, and the person you wanted to hype you actually does it. First, do a little dance, then be sure to take the time to thank him or her. When my big kahuna replied, I was shocked. I wrote him a thank-you email and a physical thank-you note that I mailed, plus a plant for his desk.

Then share your endorsement from the rooftops. This means sharing with friends and family, as well as on social media and a personal site. In this case, this endorsement would be included in a document to be shared with a small audience and not a public one. When I did eventually get the project, the person who hired me made a comment about who I had gotten to endorse me and what a big deal it was. I knew it was the right thing to have made the ask.

## The Brag Breakdown with Cleo Kim: Visibility Is Critical

*For Cleo Kim, platform strategist at the Medici Group and a trans woman, diversity and visibility are her life's work.*

### Diversity Brings Richness

"If people are coming from similar backgrounds, similar experiences, similar education, [it's likely their] ideas are fairly similar. Immediately, as soon as you bring in somebody who grew up in a different country, or in a different city, or in a different region in the United States, they already have a richness of a different experience pool. Add another dimension of diversity—whether it's gender, or ethnicity, or whether they were born in the US or they're an immigrant—[and] that has an exponential compounding factor. They have so many different places to access inspiration, to bring conversation to the table."

### Maximize the Uniqueness of Others

"How do we make this better? That's a question that's still vibrant in my heart and in my gut. And I'm so excited about the growing visibility and awareness that the trans community is having. . . . My specific passion, and curiosity, and past interest is to uplift other voices in the trans community, the gender-nonconforming community of queer folk, beyond outside and different spaces to show you that trans individual who is wondering, 'What is my future going to be?'"

### It All Starts with Visibility

"My hope is that if you are trans, or anybody, you can also achieve CEO status at a Fortune 500 company or organization. You, too, can be a leader of a think tank or a globally renowned scientific research hub. What's critical is that visibility piece."

## The Rising Tide

Think about Bragging Better in a greater context—what does all of this mean for your career, and the careers of the people we work with? There is a tremendous responsibility that comes from visibility—it's a good thing, and it's a huge opportunity, for now and in the future.

### Ready, Set, Go!

- **Ask for a brag from your friends. Know what you want and know how they can help you specifically.**

# Your Brag Better Future

We are reaching the end of your Brag Better kick-start, and the beginning of bringing these skills into your career and everyday life. How exciting, potentially scary, and important. Bragging for yourself and bragging for your friends, your colleagues, and even your family is crucial to learn. I've spent this whole book arguing it. It's so important that it has an impact on the world and the future. This takes time to develop, so be easy on yourself.

I hope that if you take nothing else from this book, that you at least take away a sense of pride in your work and in yourself. We need you to be proud of what you've done, and we need your voice. We need all of you. Thinking nobody needs to hear from you is a dangerous (and false) belief that you have internalized. Get that outta your head.

The practice of raising the voices of The Qualified Quiet will positively impact our ongoing conversations and social issues. By raising your voice, and doing so with candor, pride, strategy, and consideration, you will impact generations to come in how they see themselves and their work, not to mention who they look to for information. By showing that a deep understanding of a subject and pride for your work are integral to a work product, you are leading by example.

These activities are difficult. Bragging Better brings up anxiety, self-doubt, and questions around whether you're good enough. You are. Your accomplishments are enough. They are worth talking about. Please go out and talk about them.

The ability to choose to raise your voice, speak louder, and be more strategic is both a privilege and a right. While it's a difficult practice, it is one that is a rarefied opportunity not afforded to many, both on a national and global scale. You have the chance, you have the ability, and you are afforded the time and effort to contribute. Many are not given this same privilege. The right to speak freely and openly is often oppressed or suppressed, by cultures, governments, and those in power. If you have the choice to Brag Better, you have freedom.

I often think about the work that I do, and as an American woman, I am particularly lucky. Despite the sexism I have encountered throughout my career, I am able to create a path and help others do so, too. As a white person, I have privilege and do not have to navigate structural inequality and racism. It's a fairly American practice, Bragging Better, and I am free from persecution—real threats of harm to my safety or that of my family and friends—when I choose to do it. That is not true in many parts of the world.

Raise your voice because others cannot. Raise your voice because it is your duty to others whose voices can't be heard or aren't allowed to be used.

Whether it's the suppression or oppression of women all over the world, or of people of color, or of LGBTQ+ people, anyone who is an "other" is in danger and frequently silenced. Often by force. Systemic barriers are often less obvious than an outward show of force but are just as insidious and odious. The voices of the marginalized need to be heard, but this goes beyond just the ability to use your voice. We need those in power to help elevate those who are not. This is my wish for the world.

We have come to a place of shouting matches and muddling of truth because we've listened to the wrong people. We have a crisis of voice, a crisis of volume, and a crisis of knowledge. We have people who are not versed in what they are discussing becoming "experts," leaving those who are capable confused, angry, and unsure of where to start. That is where you, The Qualified Quiet, come in.

Our crisis of voice stops here. Or begins to change—we are putting thoughtful voices into the mix of those shouting.

You owe it to yourself to see where your voice can take you. You owe it to yourself to let your work shine and to propel it forward. You deserve more money, more time onstage, more time in meetings. Your voice will also inspire someone else—whether you see it or not—to use his or her voice, too.

We also have a crisis of truth—lies and deception abound from leadership and in media, and it feels like each day we get further and further from our core values of meaning and responsibility toward others.

The good news is that you've done the work to make sure that you are thoughtful in how you use your voice. Your commitment to the facts will show others, and even future generations, that putting thought and time into how you use your voice matters.

This skill—and it is a skill—requires work and commitment. Not only do you have to determine how you want to

Brag Better and what that looks like for you, but you have to practice it over and over again. It's a true long winding road.

You are not alone. You would be shocked by how many people, even some at the top you most admire, feel the exact same way that you do.

Once you learn to use your voice, though, it becomes easier to do, and easier to help others do, too. After a while, it doesn't feel like as much work as it used to.

Not only are you opening up the room to find an opportunity for you and your voice, but you're also letting others look around the room and take your lead. Use these chances to get into a conversation or to lead a conversation.

It is now your responsibility to pay it forward and to think about what your voice means for those who come after you. We are starting to hear voices rising, particularly among the newest generation of young Americans. For Gen Z, they have no option but to yell. Whether they're yelling about gun control or climate change, the youth are all right, and they are on it. It's time for the rest of us to catch up.

Are you a man reading this book? It is your responsibility to elevate the voices of women and others because you are a default we listen to. By cosigning the voices of others, you are making sure they are being heard in an environment that they otherwise would not be.

Are you a white person reading this book? It is your responsibility to elevate the voices or pass the microphone to those who are marginalized because of systemic racism and to be an ally for people of color.

Are you a straight person reading this? It is your responsibility to help amplify the stories of LGBTQ+ people around the globe. It is only when we begin to help others tell their stories and use our privilege for power that we begin to have the conversations we need. We don't need to tell their stories for them, but we need to make space for them to be able to tell their stories themselves.

What is going to move the needle on the greatest issues that we currently face? We can effect lasting change by leveraging our voices.

It is time for you to be unafraid and unabashed, too. If for no other reason, brag because it's important to get voices that know, voices that care, in on the key issues of our time. It's part of your civic duty. Brag to get yourself heard. And always vote.

This is our fight. So, go forth and Brag Better.

# Acknowledgments

There are so, so many people that helped *Brag Better* see the light of day, and I am so grateful that I finally got to write this book. To Leah Trouwborst, my editor, and the team at Portfolio and Penguin Random House, thank you. To my agent, Laura Lee Mattingly, for seeing the power in the concept and helping me make it a reality. To Kate Schatz, whose chance meeting and witness of a talk made me dust off and get back on the horse of this concept and who helped make this happen.

For my mother, Amy Nathan, the original Brag Better queen, for showing me that silence is not an option and for being a strong working mom. For my father, Howard Fineman, for passing down a love of writing, leading by example, combing hair, as well as a knack for kickers. To my brother, Nick Fineman, for always being there for me, even that one particularly embarrassing time that I won't acknowledge. Thank you for marrying the delightful Summer Delaney so that I could concentrate on writing this book and become close friends with a blonde. To Beth and Paul Schroeter and to Nate Homan and Leah Homan for talking things through. To Morgan Gerard Energy, for everything. You are my unicorn.

To Thread, a group of misfits, and my family, HTG. To the amazing organizations and groups, particularly of strong women, that helped me through the past near decade—The Li.st (Rachel Sklar and Glynnis MacNicol), La Coterie, TLM, Girl Up, Summit Series, the Wing, and others I'm sure I'm forgetting. Thank you to Sidwell Friends School, the Medill Cherub program, and the University of Pennsylvania.

To personal champions and mentors, thank you—especially Ed Mathias, Ruth Ann Harnisch, David Eisenhower, Diana Lazarus, Magdalena Rocio Krause, Rebekah Iliff, Whitney Johnson, Cindy Gallop, Dana Marlowe, and Susan McPherson.

To my friends, loves, and confidantes—José Lopéz Sanchéz, Nisha Chittal, Annie Friedman, Jo Sloame, Zach Eisenberg, Jessica Hoy, Julia Sushelsky, Morgan Olson, Tom McLeod, and Elizabeth Morgan, I am missing so many of you, I'm sure. To Brin Stevens, Amelia Showalter, Sara Stibitz, and Ann Maynard, thank you for all your help. To Gayle Neufeld, for getting me through it all. Also thank you to margaritas, SSRIs, Venice Beach, *Pride and Prejudice* (2005), and Nora Ephron.

To everyone that has hired me, fired me, championed me, or told me I couldn't do it, thank you. To the agent who told me this book idea was "good, not great," thank you, too. And to my baby girl, Bean, I love you.

For the young woman who asked me in a talk in 2015 if her dreams were maybe "too big," they are not. They never are, I promise.

# Notes

### Chapter 1: The "B" Word


**12 According to a 2012 study:** Kangas Dwyer, Karen. "Is Public Speaking Really More Feared Than Death?" *Communication Research Reports* 29, no. 2 (April 2012): 99–107.

**16 According to tech revolutionary Steve Jobs:** Gallo, Carmine. "Steve Jobs: Get Rid of the Crappy Stuff." *Forbes*, May 16, 2011. https://www.forbes.com/sites/carminegallo/2011/05/16/steve-jobs-get-rid-of-the-crappy-stuff/#38588d8a7145.


### Chapter 2: Why Is Bragging So Hard?


**24 Mighty Forces founder and president Amanda Hirsch:** "Researchers Unveil Key Findings on Female 'Self-Promotion Gap' in Honor of Women's Entrepreneurship Day." PRWeb, November 18, 2019. https://www.prweb.com/releases/researchers_unveil_key_findings_on_female_self_promotion_gap_in_honor_of_womens_entrepreneurship_day/prweb16731017.htm. See also The Self-Promotion Gap, https://www.selfpromotiongap.com.

**24 old journalism adage:** O'Toole, Garson. "Tell 'Em What You're Going to Tell 'Em; Next, Tell 'Em; Next, Tell 'Em What You Told 'Em." Quote Investigator, August 15, 2017. https://quoteinvestigator.com/2017/08/15/tell-em/.

**27 Silicon Valley darling Elizabeth Holmes:** Kulwin, Noah. "Theranos CEO Elizabeth Holmes's Five Best Cover Story Appearances, Ranked." *Vox*, October 26, 2015. https://www.vox.com/2015/10/26/11620036/theranos-ceo-elizabeth-holmess-five-best-cover-story-appearances. Weisul, Kimberly. "Why the Next Steve Jobs Will Be a Woman: A Rising

Tide of Female Founders Will Produce the Next Iconic Entrepreneur." *Inc.*, October 2015. https://www.inc.com/magazine/201510/kimberly-weisul/will-the-next-steve-jobs-be-a-woman.html.

**30 Impostor Phenomenon in High Achieving:** Anderson, L. V. "Feeling Like an Impostor Is Not a Syndrome." *Slate*, April 12, 2016. https://slate.com/business/2016/04/is-impostor-syndrome-real-and-does-it-affect-women-more-than-men.html.

**32 "The Good Wife's Guide":** Chang, Angel. "This 1955 'Good House Wife's Guide' Explains How Wives Should Treat Their Husbands." Little Things. Accessed January 16, 2020. https://www.littlethings.com/1950s-good-housewife-guide.

**32 historian and classicist Mary Beard:** Beard, Mary. "The Public Voice of Women." *London Review of Books* 36, no. 6 (March 20, 2014): 11–14. https://www.lrb.co.uk/v36/n06/mary-beard/the-public-voice-of-women.

**32 A study in *PLoS ONE*:** Anderson, Rindy C., and Casey A. Klofstad. "Preference for Leaders with Masculine Voices Holds in the Case of Feminine Leadership Roles." *PLOS One* 7, no. 12 (December 12, 2012). https://journals.plos.org/plosone/article?id=10.1371/journal.pone.0051216.

**33 trained to like lower voices:** Klofstad, Casey A., Rindy C. Anderson, and Susan Peters. "Sounds Like a Winner: Voice Pitch Influences Perception of Leadership Capacity in Both Men and Women." *Proceedings of the Royal Society B: Biological Sciences* 279, no. 1738 (2012): 2698–704. https://doi.org/10.1098/rspb.2012.0311.

## Chapter 3: Be Proud

**44 List everything: the small wins:** Klaus, Peggy. *Brag!: The Art of Tooting Your Own Horn Without Blowing It*. Boston: Grand Central Publishing, 2008.

## Chapter 4: Be Loud

**66 men rated themselves 15 points higher:** Exley, Christine, and Judd Kessler. "Why Don't Women Self-Promote as Much as Men?" *Harvard Business Review*, December 19, 2019. https://hbr.org/2019/12/why-dont-women-self-promote-as-much-as-men.

**67 gender differences in the self-presentation:** Lerchenmueller, Marc. "Gender Differences in How Scientists Present the Importance of Their Research: Observational Study." *BMJ* 367 (December 2019): 16573.

https://doi.org/10.1136/bmj.l6573. Cortes, Jan. "Men More Likely to Praise Their Scientific Work Than Women, Study Shows." *Medical Daily*, December 17, 2019. https://www.medicaldaily.com/men-more-likely-praise-scientific-work-women-study-shows-447209.

**67 backlash to bragging:** Fielding-Singh, Priya, Devon Magliozzi, and Swethaa Ballakrishnen. "Why Women Stay Out of the Spotlight at Work." *Harvard Business Review*, August 28, 2018. https://hbr.org/2018/08/why-women-stay-out-of-the-spotlight-at-work.

**74 Harvard's *Healthbeat* newsletter:** "Giving Thanks Can Make You Happier." Harvard Health Publishing. Accessed October 3, 2019. https://www.health.harvard.edu/healthbeat/giving-thanks-can-make-you-happier.

**80 sense of humor matters:** Half, Robert. "Humor in the Workplace: It's Good for Your Career and Business." Robert Half, July 23, 2018. https://www.roberthalf.com/blog/management-tips/humor-in-the-workplace-its-good-for-your-career-and-business.

**80 Bell Leadership Institute surveyed:** "Bell Leadership Study Finds Humor Gives Leaders the Edge." Bell Leadership Institute, March 2012. https://www.bellleadership.com/humor-gives-leaders-edge/.

**80 CareerBuilder survey of over:** "CareerBuilder Study Reveals Surprising Factors That Play a Part in Determining Who Gets Hired." CareerBuilder, August 28, 2013. https://www.careerbuilder.com/share/aboutus/pressreleasesdetail.aspx?sd=8/28/2013&id=pr778&ed=12/31/2013.

### Chapter 6: Résumés, Bios, Headshots, and Personal Websites

**122 Your personal website:** Frost, Aja. "Can a Personal Website Help Your Job Search?" *The Muse*. Accessed October 3, 2019. https://www.themuse.com/advice/can-a-personal-website-help-your-job-search-what-6-hiring-managers-really-think.

### Chapter 7: Introductions

**129 who wear name-brand clothing:** Nelissen, Rob M. A., and Marijn H. C. Meijers. "Social Benefits of Luxury Brands as Costly Signals of Wealth and Status." *Evolution and Human Behavior* 32, no. 5 (March 2011): 343–55. https://doi.org/10.1016/j.evolhumbehav.2010.12.002.

**129 people with glasses:** Brown, Michael, Ernesto Henriquez, and Jennifer Groscup. "The Effects of Eyeglasses and Race on Juror Decisions Involving a Violent Crime." *American Journal of Forensic Psychology* 26, no. 2 (2008): 25–43. https://www.researchgate.net/publication/22846

2377_The_Effects_of_Eyeglasses_and_Race_on_Juror_Decisions_Involving_a_Violent_Crime.

**129 attempt to sound intelligent:** Oppenheimer, Daniel M. "Consequences of Erudite Vernacular Utilized Irrespective of Necessity: Problems with Using Long Words Needlessly." *Applied Cognitive Psychology* 20, no. 2 (2006): 139–56. https://doi.org/10.1002/acp.1178.

**129 Judith Humphrey, a communications expert:** Humphrey, Judith. "Never, Ever 'Wing It.' This Is How to Prepare to Sound Spontaneous." *Fast Company*, October 4, 2018. https://www.fastcompany.com/90240947/never-ever-wing-it-this-is-how-to-prepare-to-sound-spontaneous.

**132 found that eye contact:** Fullwood, Chris, and Gwyneth Doherty-Sneddon. "Effect of Gazing at the Camera During a Video Link on Recall." *Applied Ergonomics* 37, no. 2 (2006): 167–75. https://doi.org/10.1016/j.apergo.2005.05.003.

**133 eye contact research:** Christian, Jarrett. "The Psychology of Eye Contact, Digested." *Research Digest*, British Psychological Society, November 28, 2016. https://digest.bps.org.uk/2016/11/28/the-psychology-of-eye-contact-digested/.

**133 firm handshake and interview ratings:** Stewart, Greg L., Susan L. Dustin, Murray R. Barrick, and Todd C. Darnold. "Exploring the Handshake in Employment Interviews." *Journal of Applied Psychology* 93, no. 5 (2008): 1139–46. https://doi.org/10.1037/0021-9010.93.5.1139.

**133 Research from the University of Alabama:** Chaplin, William, Jeffrey Phillips, Jonathan Brown, Nancy Clanton, and Jennifer Stein. "Handshaking, Gender, Personality, and First Impressions." *Journal of Personality and Social Psychology* 79 (2000): 110–17. https://doi.org/10.1037/0022-3514.79.1.110.

**133 business school students:** Schroeder, Juliana, Jane Risen, Francesca Gino, and Michael I. Norton. "Handshaking Promotes Cooperative Dealmaking." *SSRN*, May 29, 2014. https://doi.org/10.2139/ssrn.2443551.

### Chapter 8: Pitching

**140 dual coding theory:** "Dual-Coding Theory." Wikipedia, December 22, 2018. https://en.wikipedia.org/wiki/Dual-coding_theory.

### Chapter 9: Salary Negotiations

**157 A survey by Wells Fargo:** "Conversations About Personal Finance More Difficult Than Religion and Politics, According to New Wells Fargo Survey." Wells Fargo Newsroom, February 20, 2014. https://newsroom

.wf.com/press-release/community-banking-and-small-business/conversations-about-personal-finance-more.

**158 Younger Americans are starting to change:** "Poll: How Comfortable Are Americans Discussing Money?" Lexington Law, August 6, 2018. https://www.lexingtonlaw.com/blog/news/lets-talk-about-money-survey.html.

**164 Harris Poll commissioned:** Nakano, Chelsi. "Presentation Habits Presenters Don't Like to Admit." *Prezi Blog*, June 15, 2016. https://blog.prezi.com/presentation-habits-presenters-dont-like-to-admit/.

**164 Warren Buffett, speaking to:** Gallo, Carmine. "Billionaire Warren Buffett Says This 1 Skill Will Boost Your Career Value by 50 Percent." *Inc.*, January 5, 2017. https://www.inc.com/carmine-gallo/the-one-skill-warren-buffett-says-will-raise-your-value-by-50.html.

### Chapter 12: Facing Your Bragging Fears

**196 2017 survey by Reclaim Your Domain:** Buxton, Madeline. "The Internet Problem We Don't Talk Enough About." *Refinery29*, March 15, 2017. https://www.refinery29.com/en-us/online-harassment-statistics-infographic.

**198 According to a September Pew poll:** Konnikova, Maria. "The Psychology of Online Comments." *New Yorker*, October 23, 2013. https://www.newyorker.com/tech/annals-of-technology/the-psychology-of-online-comments.

### Chapter 14: How to Help Others Brag Better

**223 "The Self-Promotion Gap":** "The Self-Promotion Gap." Mighty Forces, Southpaw Insights, Upstream Analysis, and Grey Horse Communications. Accessed January 5, 2020. https://www.selfpromotiongap.com/home.

**224 *Harvard Business Review* roundup:** Menon, Tanya, and Leigh Thompson. "Envy at Work." *Harvard Business Review*, April 2010. https://hbr.org/2010/04/envy-at-work.

**224 longitudinal study of eighteen thousand:** Mujcic, Redzo, and Andrew J. Oswald. "Is Envy Harmful to a Society's Psychological Health and Wellbeing? A Longitudinal Study of 18,000 Adults." *Social Science & Medicine* 198 (2018): 103–11. https://doi.org/10.1016/j.socscimed.2017.12.030.

**225 Developing Shine Theory:** Sow, Aminatou, and Ann Friedman. "What Is Shine Theory?" Shinetheory.com. Accessed October 3, 2019. https://www.shinetheory.com/.

**228 A 2014 study of white-collar:** Kunze, Astrid, and Amalia Miller. "Women Helping Women? Evidence from Private Sector Data on Workplace Hierarchies." Working Paper 20761, National Bureau of Economic Research, December 2014. https://doi.org/10.3386/w20761.

**228 having work friends is good for you:** Mann, Annamarie. "Why We Need Best Friends at Work." Gallup, January 15, 2018. https://www.gallup.com/workplace/236213/why-need-best-friends-work.aspx.

**233 A 2014 study found:** Barsade, Sigal G., and Olivia A. O'Neill. "What's Love Got to Do with It? A Longitudinal Study of the Culture of Companionate Love and Employee and Client Outcomes in a Long-Term Care Setting." *Administrative Science Quarterly* 59, no. 4 (May 2014): 551–98. https://doi.org/10.1177/0001839214538636.

**234 repeating false statements:** Hasher, Lynn, David Goldstein, and Thomas Toppino. "Frequency and the Conference of Referential Validity." *Journal of Verbal Learning and Verbal Behavior* 16, no. 1 (February 1977): 107–12. https://doi.org/10.1016/S0022-5371(77)80012-1.

**236 When President Obama took office:** Eilperin, Juliet. "White House Women Want to Be in the Room Where It Happens." *Washington Post*, September 13, 2016. https://www.washingtonpost.com/news/powerpost/wp/2016/09/13/white-house-women-are-now-in-the-room-where-it-happens/.

**241 According to the *Harvard Business Review*:** Johnson, W. Brad, and David G. Smith. "How Men Can Become Better Allies to Women." *Harvard Business Review*, October 12, 2018. https://hbr.org/2018/10/how-men-can-become-better-allies-to-women.

**241 Penelope Gazin and Kate Dwyer:** Titlow, John Paul. "These Women Entrepreneurs Created a Fake Male Cofounder to Dodge Startup Sexism." *Fast Company*, August 29, 2017. https://www.fastcompany.com/40456604/these-women-entrepreneurs-created-a-fake-male-cofounder-to-dodge-startup-sexism.

**241 Social capital and elite connections:** Palgi, Michal, and Gwen Moore. "Social Capital: Mentors and Contacts." *Current Sociology* 52, no. 3 (May 2004): 459–80. https://doi.org/10.1177/0011392104043087.

**242 never do an all-male panel:** Collins, Francis S. "Time to End the Manel Tradition." National Institutes of Health, US Department of Health and Human Services, June 12, 2019. https://www.nih.gov/about-nih/who-we-are/nih-director/statements/time-end-manel-tradition.

# Index